CHILTERNS TO THE
WELSH BORDERS

EXPLORING WOODLAND

WOODLAND
TRUST

CHILTERNS TO THE
WELSH BORDERS

Edited by Lorraine Weeks & Graham Blight

FRANCES LINCOLN LIMITED
PUBLISHERS

Acknowledgements

Introduction by Archie Miles
Site entries written by Sheila Ashton
Researched by Lorraine Weeks, Tim Hill, Lesley Silvera & Diana Moss
Edited by Lorraine Weeks & Graham Blight
Maps by Linda M Dawes, Belvoir Cartographics & Design

Photographic acknowledgements

Alec Connah: 83, Archie Miles: 15, 16, 103, 116, 129,
Avon Wildlife Trust: 121, Bob Corns, English Nature: 125
Bucks, Berks and Oxon Wildlife Trust: 39, 43 (Jim Asher), 44 (Jim Asher)
Claire Adams: 119, Colm O' Kelly: 8, Corporation of London: 29
Forestry Commission: 40, 56, 57, Lorraine Weeks: 1, 80, 89, 99, 100, 104
National Trust: 92 (David Noton), 93, 109 (Nick Meers),
Queenswood Country Park: 97, The Gerald Palmer Eling Trust: 21,
The Parks Trust, Milton Keynes: 52, Warwickshire Wildlife Trust: 66, 68, 72,
Woodland Trust: 2, 26, 27, 31, 58, 60, 75, 76, 86 (Jane Button), 101, 105, 106,
    107, 114
Worcestershire Wildlife Trust: 74

Frances Lincoln Ltd
4 Torriano Mews
Torriano Avenue
London NW5 2RZ
www.franceslincoln.com

Chilterns to the Welsh Borders
Copyright © Frances Lincoln 2006
Text © Woodland Trust 2006

First Frances Lincoln edition: 2006

A catalogue record for this book is available
from the British Library.

ISBN 10: 0-7112-2601-6
ISBN 13: 978-0-7112-2601-2

Printed and bound in Singapore
The paper used in this book was sourced from
sustainable forests, managed according to FSC
(Forest Stewardship Council) guidelines.

1 2 3 4 5 6 7 8 9

Half title page Croft Woodlands

Title page Foxgloves at Pepper Wood

Contents

How to use this guide

Covering a region that encompasses the Chilterns to the Cotswolds and along the Severn and Wye valleys to the Welsh Borders. This book is divided into four areas represented by key maps on pages 18-19, 48-49, 70-71 and 94-95. The tree symbols on these maps denote the location of each wood. In the pages following the key maps, the sites nearest one another are described together (wherever practical) to make planning a day out as rewarding as possible.

For each site entry the name of the nearest town/village is given, followed by road directions and the grid reference of the site entrance. The area of the site (in hectares followed by acres) is given together with the official status of the site where appropriate and the owner, body or organisation responsible for maintaining the site. Symbols are used to denote information about the site and its facilities as explained in the next column.

Symbols used denote information about each site and the facilities to be found there.

Type of wood

Mainly broadleaved woodland
Mainly coniferous woodland
Mixed woodland

Car park

Parking on site
Parking nearby
Parking difficult to find

Official status

Area of Outstanding Natural Beauty
AONB
Site of Special Scientific Interest SSSI

Site facilities

Sign at entry
Information board
One or more paths suitable for
  wheelchair users
Dogs allowed under supervision
Waymarked trail
Toilet
Picnic area
Entrance/car park charge
Refreshments on site

7

Chilterns to the Welsh Borders

Bluebells, Blaise Castle

Think of the Chilterns and their woodlands and the first word that comes to mind must be 'beech'. It could be those smooth, grey, elephantine boles gilded by the low-level sunlight of a late winter's day, the emerald ocean-wave canopy swaying rhythmically overhead in spring, or the burnished gold of autumn's fire – a glow to cheer the departing year and soon to fall into deep drifts ripe for running and tumbling.

Heading northeast from the M4 corridor the hills and vales of East Oxfordshire, Berkshire and Buckinghamshire boast many fine beech woods, and some startlingly beautiful and varied sites among them. In a region of Britain which has been under increasing pressure for development and agricultural improvement over the last 50 years it's pretty remarkable that so much woodland has survived, in no short measure due to the indefatigable work of the Wildlife Trusts, Woodland Trust and various local authorities and private owners. Once these were all working woodlands, in particular providing beech timber and beechwood products, such as chair legs and spindles, turned by the hundreds of 'bodgers' who lived and worked in the woods, for the nearby furniture industry centred around High

Wycombe. A few woods have once more begun to be worked for their coppice products, but in general the legacy is a delightful collection of fine amenity woodlands.

A little way along the M4 from London, near Slough, is Burnham Beeches, one of the most exceptional sites for truly ancient beech trees in the whole of Britain. Many of the massive old pollards here will be in excess of 400 years old, and there are more than 450 of these precarious old stagers to be discovered all over this ancient wood pasture and common. In the 17th century it has been estimated that there were some 3,000 such trees here and back in 1737 Thomas Gray (he of *Elegy in a Country Churchyard*) was moved to write in a letter to Horace Walpole.... 'Both hill and vale are covered with most venerable Beeches, and other reverend vegetables that, like most other ancient people, are always dreaming out their old stories to the winds.' Perhaps the most famous of the lot is the Cage Pollard, which featured back in 1990 as a backdrop to scenes in the movie *Robin Hood Prince of Thieves*. A regular pollarding regime would have been in place for about 300 years up until about 1820. In 1880 the Corporation of London (still the current owner) bought the site as a public open space for Londoners, and thus it has remained. The gales of 1987 and 1990 took their toll on the great old trees, but continuing care and management, which includes the cautious re-pollarding of some trees, sees them set for another century or two yet.

Driving north from the M4, towards High Wycombe, few motorists would give a second glance to a steep wooded hillside bordering the Thames near Marlow, but it's well worth finding the time to park and explore the splendid Bisham Woods. It's hard to escape the nearby roar of traffic, but drop down into some of the old paths and sunken tracks and discover the wood which inspired Kenneth Grahame's Wild Wood in *The Wind in the Willows*, and find that even today this is still a magical place. Recognised as one of Berkshire's richest ancient woodlands it's possible to find about 50 ancient woodland indicator plants here. The beeches sway gently in the breeze high overhead, but there is also alder in the wetter parts and coppiced hazel and hornbeam. Bisham is a haven of green sanity, caught between the roar of traffic and the imminent sprawl of London commuterland, increasingly vital in the 21st century.

Escape further from the Metropolis to the very western escarpment of the Chilterns, and be astounded that around 40 years ago the Highways Authority won the right to gouge the M40 through the hills above Watlington, and what is now the Aston Rowant National Nature Reserve. Again, the roar of the traffic may be a little intrusive, but if for nothing else alone this is the best place in England to come and watch the glorious red kites leisurely wheeling over the chalky slopes; the stars of a reintroduction programme which has spectacularly exceeded the hopes of all those concerned. Lying on your back on Bald Hill, amid the fragrant junipers, you'll get the most laid back aerial acrobatic display ever as the kites leisurely flick their triangular tails this way and that as they cruise left and right seeking some hapless rodent scurrying below. With patience you may well have these birds flying barely 30 or 40 feet above you, and it's not uncommon to see at least half a dozen at a time. Incidentally, there is also some very interesting woodland here too, with ash, beech, yew and whitebeam of all shapes and sizes growing over ancient tracks, banks and ditches. There are great shows of flowers on the chalk slopes – Chiltern gentian being one of the rarer specialities. On top of the hill and across the other side of the road to Christmas Common lies Cowleaze Wood – a different prospect indeed. Lots of wide rides and good footpaths through stands of conifers, oak coppice, some handsome beeches as well as an ever-changing collection of woodland sculptures along a marked trail.

Adding new dimensions to the woodland experience is a great way of enticing more people to visit. At King's Wood, on the urban fringe of High Wycombe, there has been a concerted effort to mesh recreational amenity with good management and wildlife conservation. There are paths and rides in abundance, and a selection of permanent orienteering courses have also been marked out with a special map also available for participants, more encouragement to get fit whilst enjoying woodland. Principally a beech with oak wood, there's history in the ancient boundary banks, butterflies and

Cowleaze Wood, Watlington

birds to watch out for and recently created ponds where broad-bodied chaser dragonflies patrol above frogs and common newts.

If it's activity you're after then the Forestry Commission can give you plenty of that in its Wendover Wood, near Aylesbury. Again, an orienteering course is on the menu, but you could also mountain bike, horse ride, climb on (and possibly fall off – don't worry, there's a soft landing) some of the climbing frames and swings. Exhausted? Rustle up a barbecue on one of the permanent stands provided and afterwards take a quiet stroll and try to spot the elusive little firecrest – Europe's smallest bird, at a mere nine centimetres long and weighing no more than a ten pence piece.

At the northern extremity of the Chilterns, as Buckinghamshire gives way to Hertfordshire, mention must be made of the Ashridge Estate – once again a smashing place for a great family day out, as there's such a great sense of space here – over 4,000 acres to explore. Ashridge it may be by name, but once again beech is in command, and to be found in all shapes and sizes, from lofty and vibrant plantations through to the decrepit old pollards and coppice stools which stand sentinel along many of the ancient boundary banks and trackways. Ashridge is steeped in history. The prehistoric Icknield Way runs along a contour of the hillside. The monument in the centre of the park commemorates the Duke of Bridgewater, who built the first canal. Capability Brown helped to shape the parkland landscape and there is one of the country's oldest surviving post mills here too.

Northamptonshire and Warwickshire may not immediately seem to offer a plethora of ancient woodland, and yet there are still a few gems to be discovered. In Northants. the woodland at Everdon Stubbs, near Daventry, holds many signs of its ancient origins; banks and ditches galore and a large holloway. The wood has been documented since the 10th century, and there is thought to be part of a prehistoric burial site on its northern boundary. Fine trees include hornbeam and sweet chestnut coppice stools in this predominantly oak with birch wood. The floral treat here is the springtime display of wild daffodils – the best to be found in the county. In Warwickshire it's always worth a trip to Ryton Wood for superb carpets of anemones and bluebells spiked with red campion, violets and, in the shadier spots, the delicate little wood sorrel. This part oak-hazel and part oak-lime wood is also home to nightingales and the rare white admiral butterfly.

If it's those great open spaces which bring that refreshment and elevation to the soul which we all crave then the Wyre Forest is an ideal place to head. The Wyre is one of the largest semi-natural ancient woodlands in lowland England and has a rich working history. For hundreds of years its coppice oak woods proved invaluable in charcoal production for the West Midlands iron industry and seasonal gangs of tan bark workers came in the spring to strip the oak bark which was indispensable for the leather industry. Today, a little coppicing and even bark peeling still continues, but most of the demand in the leather industry has been eclipsed by synthetic chemicals. Careful exploration will uncover some of this working woodland heritage and, with luck and a bit of guidance, it's well worth trying to find one of Britain's rarest native trees – the whitty pear, or true service tree – a solitary specimen of which is standing in the depths of the forest. Although this actual tree is only 90 years old, it is known to be a direct descendant of an ancient specimen which was recorded in 1678, but lost to a malicious fire in 1862. The species is only known in a very few other sites around Britain.

Thinking of woodland in the 20th century, the sad fact is that much of it was lost to agricultural improvement and, where industry was concerned, it was the very lack of woodmanship that left many old woods to revert into tangled jungles where the biodiversity was squeezed out. In recent years Worcestershire Wildlife Trust was fortunate enough to acquire Trench Wood near Grimley and Monkwood near Droitwich, which had been under the ownership of the nearby Harris Brush Company and worked as coppice until the 1960s. Obviously plastic ousted wood in the brush-making industry, but it meant that these and nearby Offmoor Wood had remained as vibrant wildlife habitats due to the management regime, and man's intervention had done no harm to the many species of birds, butterflies and plants therein.

To the west of Birmingham much of Shropshire provides essential green respite for Brummies. As a county, and considering its very rural and sparsely populated character, Shropshire is not greatly endowed with ancient woodland, but what does survive is typified by coppice sessile oakwoods, and perhaps one of the best of these is Helmeth Wood, above Church Stretton. It's a bit of a hike up the hill, but in spring the heady scent of the bluebells will draw you on, and reaching the crest you can marvel at the twisted and tortured forms of the old oak coppice stools, some of them almost three metres in diameter.

Dropping down into Herefordshire lays temptation in the path of your author, for this is his adopted home of the last 14 years and with obvious reason he could wax lyrically about every wooded corner of the county. The diversity here is manifold, from the glorious wooded parkland of Croft Castle in the north to the romance and drama of the Wye Valley woods. Credenhill is worth mentioning, as it is one of the Woodland Trust's most recent acquisitions and, although currently swathed in the gloomy mantle of commercial conifers, there will be a renaissance as they make way for the broadleaves to dominate once again. The revelation of rediscovering the Iron Age hill fort that lurks beneath also awaits the visitor. Some ancient and picturesque yews still cling to these old ramparts.

Croft is a must. Here the struggle between commercial forestry and ancient trees is enacted once again. In the Forestry Commission's softwood plantations of the 1940s and 50s, which border the old parkland, remnant boles of massive old oaks and chestnuts can be glimpsed, appearing ghostlike beneath the western hemlocks, many of the latter with the impudence to set their seeds in the crooks and hollows of the deceased veterans. Time was when the Forestry Commission did their utmost to eradicate these old trees. How times change (thank goodness)! Both the F.C. and Croft's owners, the National Trust, are doing all in their power to nurture the veteran survivors in both the open parkland and woodland clearings. Britain's only triple avenue of sweet chestnuts has been here for about 450 years and, although storm and disease has taken its toll, looks set for another century or two still.

In the far south of the county and only separated from Gloucestershire and the Forest of Dean by the width of the river Wye, lies Little Doward; one of the flagship woods of the amazing woodland network of the Lower Wye Valley. This isn't easy walking – the hill is steep, but the rewards are easily worth the struggle. Little Doward was once largely a deer park and moves are afoot to restore that situation, including the removal of most of the conifers from its commercial past. The tree celebrities here are the beeches – giant pollards and coppice stools, long neglected, but startlingly beautiful. At the top of the hill, and hidden in much the same fashion as Credenhill, is another giant Iron Age hill fort, whose perfect strategic position can be well appreciated by its commanding views down the Wye valley far below. Your walk back downhill, around the precipitous limestone crags, is overhung with yews, rare limes and whitebeams thrusting improbably from the bare rockface.

Hop aboard the old ropeway ferry at Symonds Yat and you're soon in the Gloucestershire side of the Wye valley woodland system. With patience you can explore and discover some awesome remnants of the Wye's industrial and natural history heritage. In the Forest of Dean itself there is plenty of good even-aged forestry which is still regularly worked, and within this there's loads of space for biking, riding and walking, not to mention the famous and, arguably one of the country's best, Sculpture Trail. Along the Wye valley, where the steep hillsides made modern forestry difficult, some fascinating reminders of a way of life long gone linger on. In Cadora Woods it's very easy to spot numerous small, level platforms about the hillside, which were once cut out to be used as charcoal hearths. A gentle

Sculpture Trail, Forest of Dean

scrape of the boot will unearth the dense black dust still packed on the earth and suddenly an image is conjured of the valley wreathed in the smoke of the old earthburns and ringing with the blows of the woodman's axe. There are many mighty old small-leaved lime and ash coppice stools in these woods, which must have been cut over the centuries, but have now stood unworked for over a 100 years.

Another woodland just over the Herefordshire/Gloucestershire border is Dymock Wood. On the map it might not look promising as the M50 ploughs right through it. Even so, this is a wood which has plenty to offer – fen, acid marsh, streams, ponds and heathland and, on bordering land, some superb old hedgerows and traditional orchards. However, the absolute jewel in this woodland crown is the stunning and nationally unrivalled display of wild daffodils in the spring.

Westonbirt Arboretum

Again, Gloucestershire throws up so many wonderful woods it's difficult to know where to stop, but a trawl along the western escarpment of the Cotswolds reveals several splendid examples – Siccaridge and Sapperton Valley, Midger and just above Cheltenham the delights of Lineover Wood – lots of good beech here, but also small-leaved lime and oak with the occasional whitebeam and field maple.

For a cracking day out and a veritable feast of trees both native and introduced, nothing beats the Forestry Commission's Westonbirt Arboretum, near Tetbury – frankly the best arboretum in the land. There's everything here, including Silk Wood with its 2,000+ year old small-leaved lime stool, hundreds of British record breakers, rarities from every corner of the globe (what better place to study a tree species you're thinking of planting, and see how it turns out), a fantastic colour blast of exotic acers in the autumn, and even floodlit evening displays. Trees and plants are available to buy at the nursery and there are lots of annual special events.

Most of this guidebook has managed to skirt skilfully around the major cities, but lands full square on Bristol in the southwestern quarter. Although many woods are to be found around the city, the area as a whole was designated as one of the 12 Community Forests of England back in 1992, and covers 221 square miles around Bristol. A partnership of local authorities, conservation NGOs and a host of local communities, farmers, landowners and businesses are pulling together to transform and improve the area. In essence the Great Western Community Forest creates new woodland and sustainably manages existing woodland for its amenity value, commercial viability and landscape, heritage and biodiversity benefits. This contributes to an improved quality of life for all, encourages businesses and inward investment and furthers the conservation of wildlife and landscape character within the region.

One of the most spectacular of Bristol's many woodlands is Leigh Woods, set high above the Avon Gorge, which is accessible for all with its broad paths. Walkers, cyclists or even wheelchair-users will soon appreciate the splendour of this fine old wood. Limes, both small-leaved and large-leaved, are here, as well as some very large wild service trees and rare whitebeams, although these are principally on the steeper cliffs above the Gorge (take great care). In nearby Ashton Court there are some massive old oaks to be found in a beautifully maintained parkland setting, but for a contrasting taste of the really wild try Weston Big Wood, a few miles down the road, near Portishead. Narrow paths weave through this maze of ash and lime in an untouched woodland where non-intervention has been the policy. Wind-fallen giants scatter the ground, some regenerating upwards again from prone, or springing anew from partially dislodged rootplates. If, as many do, they die and rot they provide wonderful deadwood habitat for all manner of invertebrates and fungi. This is a wood for all the senses – and a good sense of direction in addition is very helpful.

The variety of woodland within the scope of this particular guidebook, given the geographical spread and the diversity of the landscape, should keep you entertained with woodland ramblings for a goodly while, so pull the old walking boots on and get out there and enjoy it come rain or shine.

ARCHIE MILES

MAP 1

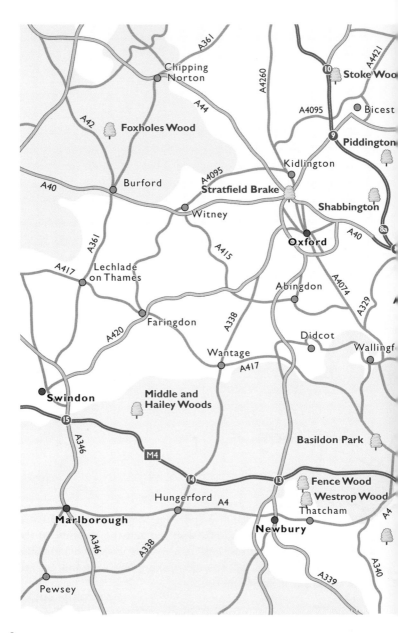

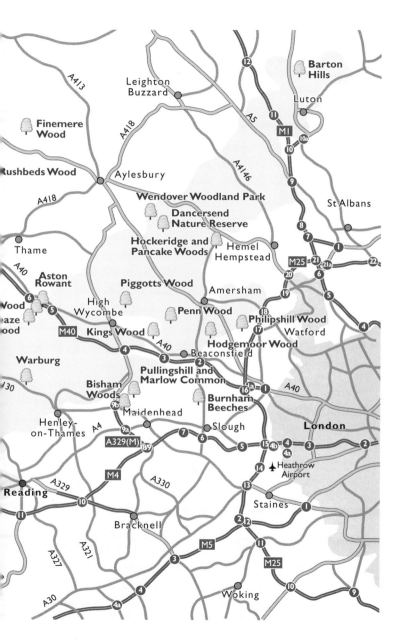

MAP 1

Middle & Hailey Woods
Lambourn

4km (2.5miles) south of Ashbury,
5.5km (3.5 miles) north of
Lambourn on west side of the
B4000. (SU283824)
40ha (99acres), SSSI

The National Trust

These two woods lying in a big,
wide, open valley in the heart of
horse riding and racing country,
provide a real contrast: one full
of grandeur, the other a more
sober plantation.

The sites are bisected by a broad
grass avenue and a series of
sinuous rides and glades offering
glimpses of romantic 17th-century
Ashdown House.

Here was once a 14th-century
medieval park that provided the
Abbot of Glastonbury with a
valuable source of venison. Today,
part of the estate is a site of special
scientific interest thanks to the
geology of the sandstone over
chalk, and rich lichen growth.

Alive with plants and animals, the
woods house wild fallow deer,
three species of woodpecker,
buzzards and red kites, redpoll and
occasionally crossbill. Purple
hairstreak and brimstone butterflies
can be seen here, while herb paris,
saxifrage, primroses and snowdrops
add colour at ground level.

While the woods and downland
are closed on Fridays, access paths
remain open.

Westrop Wood
Newbury

From A4 at Thatcham follow signs
to Cold Ash. After 1.5km (1mile)
turn right into Bucklebury Alley.
Follow road for 500m (0.5 mile) to
wood entrance on right at double
gates set back from road.
(SU517708), 25ha (62acres)

Mr Constantinidi

Slightly unkempt but with a
charm that creeps up on you
unawares, this is a fun wood to
explore for those willing to take
on the task of navigation.

An absence of signs shouldn't
deter the visitor with a good sense
of direction and the slightly untidy
look belies the care lavished on it
in the past.

Almost an urban-fringe wood,
the site links with more extensive
woodland sandwiched between
the River Pang and the Kennet

and Avon Canal.

Once inside, it has a very different character, with a commercial conifer plantation quickly giving way to mixed broadleaves – and the diversity of habitats in such a relatively small area not only impresses, but is also a delight for the senses.

One minute you are walking through dense western hemlock, the next perched on a knoll surrounded by stately beech, oak and Scots pine or tripping over wood banks and squelching through groves of alder, willow and aspen.

Fence Wood
Thatcham

Heading north on B4009 in Hermitage, turn right signposted Bucklebury, Marlston and Frilsham. Go under disused railway bridge, up hill, and down other side. Bottom of hill, car park on right opposite Frilsham turn.

(SU513723), 152ha (376acres), AONB

The Gerald Palmer Eling Trust

Historic links, impressive views and an ever-changing landscape ▸▸

Fence Wood

MAP 1

await visitors to Fence Wood.

But the jewel in its crown is the impressive Iron Age hill fort of Grimsbury Castle whose surviving banks, ramparts and ditches overlook the Kennet and Pang valleys.

A good choice of tracks and paths allow exploration of the spruce-dominated coniferous woodland – with its Scots pine and Lawson cypress – and wetter areas with alder, birch and ancient woodland remnants.

Much of the site is operated commercially and certified for sustainable management. The stone ride climbs dramatically through newly-planted woodland to mature oaks and beech where extensive earthworks are unveiled.

Complement your visit with a walk through neighbouring Down and Park woods, contrasting sites separated by a wood bank. Park Wood is dominated by conifers with a smattering of sycamore while the ancient woodland site of Down Wood boasts some magnificent hilltop veteran oaks and Pang valley views.

Ufton Wood
Reading

A4 west of Theale, turn south towards Ufton Nervet, crossing the Kennet and Avon Canal, through the village passing between the woods, turn right at T junction and right again at crossroads. Car park on right under height barrier.
(SU628652), 165ha (408acres)
Englefield Estate Office

A working wood – with timber production literally at its heart – Ufton Wood has much to attract the visitor, including an open welcome.

On the many tracks and routes through the site you are likely to encounter evidence of its ancient links – a Roman road ran through nearby Ufton Nervet. An impressively large section of the pre-Roman 'Grims' Bank' extends through the wood and its route is echoed by one of the tracks.

The centre is dominated by conifers, in particular Scots pine, spruce and larch, providing colour, texture and shade. Visit in winter and you're likely to encounter log piles and hear a chainsaw at work.

It's a little quieter in the wet flushes and around the spring-fed oval pond where alder and willow thrive and the spring water bubbles through a weir before flowing into streams.

Basildon Park
Reading

A329 between Goring and
Pangbourne, follow signs to
car park.
(SU609784)
77ha (190acres)

The National Trust

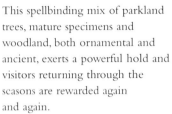

This spellbinding mix of parkland
trees, mature specimens and
woodland, both ornamental and
ancient, exerts a powerful hold and
visitors returning through the
seasons are rewarded again
and again.

Far and away the main attraction
is the abundance of mature
specimen trees – a backdrop of
elegant beech, ash, oak and sweet
chestnut intermingled with cherry,
yew, lime, maple and holly.

While the storm of 1990 took its
toll here, new planting and
regeneration has quickly filled
the gaps, breathing new life into
the landscape.

The grounds were designed to
be admired from the beautiful
Palladian mansion but the reverse
is just as true and glimpses of the
house and pleasure grounds add to
your woodland walk.

The park is managed to encourage
insects, birds and mammals, while
bluebells and yellow archangel
flourish on old earth banks in this
ancient woodland.

MAP 1

Warburg Reserve
Henley-on-Thames

6.4km (4 miles) northwest of Henley-on-Thames. From B480 in Middle
Assendon, take narrow lane signposted Bix Bottom, just north of the
Rainbow pub. Follow twisty lane along valley bottom. On reaching a small
grassy triangle, follow the road round to the right. After 1.5km (1 mile)
car park on right.

(SU720880), 109 ha, (267acres), AONB, SSSI

The Berkshire, Buckinghamshire & Oxfordshire Wildlife Trust

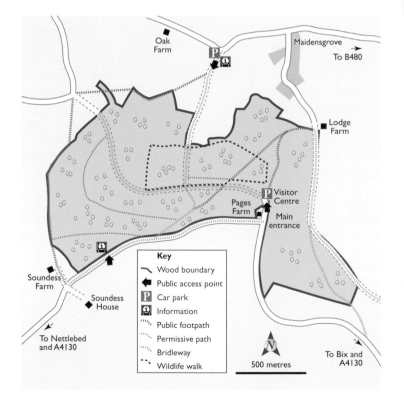

Key

⌒ Wood boundary
◀ Public access point
P Car park
ℹ Information
···· Public footpath
···· Permissive path
···· Bridleway
- - Wildlife walk

500 metres

Oak Farm

Maidensgrove
To B480

Lodge Farm

Visitor Centre
Pages Farm
Main entrance

Soundess Farm
Soundess House

To Nettlebed
and A4130

To Bix and
A4130

Warburg Reserve

Justifiably a showpiece reserve, this is a site to be savoured.

Set in a quiet Chiltern backwater – just four miles from Henley-on-Thames – even the approach is stunning, with wonderful views across the valley, to wooded slopes, pasture and carefully tended arable fields.

This reserve is a delight to the senses, with aromatic herbs crushed underfoot, the meadow a riot of colour and nectar for insects, birds, mammals and invertebrates. On a hot summer day, you may glimpse lizards, slow-worms and snakes in the grassy margins.

Scattered, informal signs provide valuable hints of treasures to look out for and are an inspiration for young visitors.

A winding path through a newer section opens into an area of ancient woodland with beech, hornbeam, oak, yew and ash. A significant number of planted conifers have been retained within the woodland and these are helping to sustain populations of goldcrest, crossbills, kestrels and sparrow hawks.

This year-round destination has a huge array of flora including less common plants such as green hellebore, Chiltern gentian, three different species of helleborine and bird's nest orchid. In autumn it provides a phenomenal display of fruiting fungi – more than 900 species have been recorded.

And if all this is not enough to keep even the most curious visitor intrigued for the day, it is possible to combine this visit with a walk or cycle ride along the footpaths of the Chilterns and Oxfordshire Way or a visit to nearby Stonor Park.

MAP 1

Pullingshill & Marlow Common

Marlow

South from High Wycombe on A404 take A4155 to Marlow centre following signs to Henley. As the A4155 comes out of the town, turn right signposted Marlow Common. Follow this road for 1km (0.5mile) and, at fork, bear right onto road that runs through wood. Parking along this road. (SU863861), 27ha (68 acres), SSSI

Woodland Trust

Part of a large area of woodland, this easy to access site is a well-loved and much-used amenity.

The wood itself has been designated both a site of special scientific interest and a special area of conservation because of the rich and diverse ground flora.

Despite suffering in the storms of 1987 and 1990 there are encouraging signs of natural regeneration with birch and beech on the plateau and ash dominating the lower slopes.

The planted wooded common is dotted with pits and hollows and boasts an enviable variety of unusual plants.

The wood bank separating Pullingshill Wood from the common indicates the ancient boundary between Great Marlow and Medenham parishes. Look out too for World War One trenches – a legacy of when this wood was used as a practice area.

From the minute you step out of the car, you quickly realise why so many people come here.

Pullingshill Wood

Bisham Woods

Bisham Woods
Cookham Dene

South from High Wycombe on A404 take M155 to centre of Marlow. At roundabout, take first exit for Bisham. After crossing suspension bridge over the Thames, turn left into Quarry Wood Road. Follow to top of hill then right into Grubwood Lane. Several parking places on right. (SU852844), 153ha (378acres)

Woodland Trust

There are two compelling reasons to visit Bisham woods, a series of vertiginous beechwoods bordering the Thames near Marlow.

One is that they are the richest ancient woods in Berkshire, a place of piled leaves, mossed banks and holes, fallen trunks, chalk banks and quarries, and hazel and hornbeam coppice. Rare helleborine orchids, thin-spiked sedge, wood barley, tutsan, nettle-leaved bellflower and goldilocks buttercup are among about 50 plants pointing to the woods' ancient origins, while an interesting collection of snails are another indicator of their great diversity. It all adds up to the fact that Bisham Woods are almost certainly remnants of the original wildwood that once covered Britain.

This leads to the second reason for pausing in this particular spot, for Bisham Woods were the inspiration for the Wild Wood in Kenneth Grahame's classic children's book *The Wind in the Willows*.

Access is via an extensive network of paths, bridleways and footpaths, ideal for walkers and riders.

MAP 1

Burnham Beeches
Beaconsfield & Slough

Main access off A355 Slough to Beaconsfield road, between the two pubs 'The Royal Oak' and 'The Foresters'. Turn into Beeches Road and continue for 400m (0.25 mile).

(SU953850), 220ha (544acres)

Corporation of London

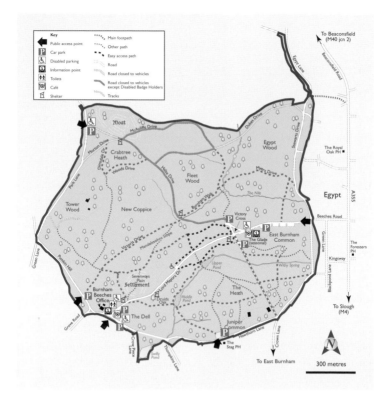

Burnham Beeches

A stunning woodland mix of oak, beech pollards and one of Britain's most spectacular wood pastures, Burnham Beeches are woods to visit time and time again.

Mature trees, boasting quaint names and histories, date back some 500 years or more. They have been allowed to develop into unique wildlife habitats, thanks to a well-thought-out management system. Traditional techniques – including grazing by Berkshire pigs and British white cattle – are being reintroduced to prolong the life of these veteran trees.

Exquisite extra details, such as elegant wrought-iron marker posts, simply add to the delight of a visit.

Each twist and turn of the formal and informal paths leads through heathland, mire and wetland to reveal an ever-changing character and atmosphere. A host of archaeological features, from wood banks and ponds to glades, moats and dells can be seen along the way.

Burnham Beeches' status as a National Nature Reserve and Special Area of Conservation recognises its international importance as a wildlife conservation area. Visitors are asked to abide by the site's byelaws and must keep dogs under control at all times.

MAP 1

Hodgemoor Wood
Chalfont St Giles

Turn of A355 between Amersham and Beaconsfield opposite Mulberry Bush pub (Bottrells Lane). Car park 1.5km (1 mile) on right.
(SU967938), 118ha (292acres), SSSI
Forestry Commission

The Chiltern Heritage Trail runs through this distinctive woodland, whose very name, based on the Saxon 'Hodd', meaning folk of the area, evokes a long and varied history.

Records date Hodgemoor Wood back to the 13th century and the presence of wood banks, venerable pollarded hornbeam, sunken tracks and chalk and flint pits affirm a wealth of uses, underlining its ancient origins.

Walkers can draw year-round access, thanks to a network of footpaths, permissive bridleways and a waymarked trail. These lead to a central ancient woodland core.

Oak and beech dominate but there are also extensive ash and hornbeam stands with groves of cherry and aspen on more fertile and wetter sections. Below these taller trees is a dense shrub layer of thorn, hazel, field maple, birch and holly. Young birch and oak are already emerging following felling of spruce and pine planting.

Philipshill Wood
Chorleywood

Turn off A404 at traffic lights toward Chorleywood Station. Pass station on left and under railway line joining Shire Lane. At top of hill road bends sharply to left, but take the turning ahead into Old Shire Lane. Spaces to park in lane after it turns to dirt track.
(TQ010947), 31ha (77acres), AONB
Woodland Trust

A treasure trove of stunning wildflowers typical of ancient woodland sites can be found just minutes from the urban sprawl of London.

Philipshill Wood boasts bluebell, wood anemone, wood sorrel, wood spurge, wood mellic and several species of orchid, and offers welcome and quiet seclusion for local people who visit the site regularly for walks.

This woodland was cleared and planted with beech and conifers in the late 1960s. Young beech, which was once produced commercially on this site, now dominates.

A green lane, known as Old Shire Lane, running on the eastern boundary of the wood is believed to be part of the ancient boundary separating Wessex and Mercia. Other ancient earthworks can be found in the wood plus a boundary stone which is likely to be glacial.

Penn Wood
Penn Street, Nr. Amersham

South of A404, between High Wycombe and Amersham. Reaching Penn Street, park adjacent to the Common/Cricket Ground on main street. Take care not to obstruct access to houses. (SU914959)
177ha (437acres), AONB
Woodland Trust

In an area renowned for its rich stock of ancient woodland, Penn Wood, at its very heart, stands out as one of the largest.

The wood forms part of a mosaic of semi-natural ancient woodland and wood pasture, grassland and scrub, rich in wildlife and flora including at least ten plants not commonly found in the county. It has a good bird population and a number of nationally scarce invertebrates.

Some of its older inhabitants include the remains of an ancient beech and a veteran oak, along with a scattering of trees dating back more than 200 years.

Archaeological features dot the site, among them wood banks, flint and clay pits.

A community group, who successfully fought off attempts to develop a golf course on the site remain as helpful guardians today. Penn Wood is well served with a network of paths.

Penn Wood

MAP 1

Kings Wood
High Wycombe

From centre of High Wycombe take A40 east for 3km (2 miles) turn left into Cock Lane. 2.5km (1.5 miles) to edge of Tylers Green. Kings Wood accessed from layby on left just past first house. (SU891941), 75ha (186acres)

Wycombe Parish Council

Well used and treasured by local people, this beech-dominated woodland sits on the crest of a hill overlooking High Wycombe.

The wood has been worked by man for centuries and remains in active management today, a fact sometimes difficult to believe in this tranquil setting with its quiet trackways.

Oak, ash and cherry flourish here, along with holly, thorn and a grove of coppiced whitebeam.

Several wood banks, often topped by veteran beech, can be seen – notably along the southern edge. Within the wood the 1987 storm opened up areas to create new habitats such as glades and wide rides, encouraging a diversity of plants, mammals and birds.

Many features of the wood have evocative names: Chepping Ponds, Heartbreak Hill, Yaffle Glade and Brian's Bridge. These can all be seen on a circular walk.

Piggotts Wood
High Wycombe

Take A4128 north of High
Wycombe for 3km (2 miles). Stay
in Hughenden valley, and after
another 1.5km (1 mile) turn left at
the Harrow pub towards Speen.
At North Dean turn right
up narrow and steep track to
Piggotts Hill. Park at top on right
in layby, opposite Glasyers.
(SU853987), 20ha (49acres),
AONB

Dr N Wheeler Robinson

A visit to Piggotts Wood is to be
savoured even before you arrive,
since the journey is a delight,
through valleys seemingly
untouched by time.

The semi-natural ancient
woodland is managed for recreation
and wildlife but there is evidence
of a vibrant and varied woodland
industry, including the remains of
30 old sawpits, charcoal hearths and
quarries. There are many old tracks
and boundary banks, lynchets, and
at least two sites with evidence of
early (Iron Age) metal-working.
Over the last decade thinning,
felling and replanting have added to
its diversity.

Most of the beech was first
planted in the 18th century for
the local furniture industry and
statuesque trees give the margins
of the wood an open feel,
providing views across the valley.

Higher up are young ash, beech,
cherry and oak with a dense
understorey of birch, holly and
hazel. Botanists may note coralroot
bittersweet, yellow bird's nest,
violet helleborine and green
hellebore. Red kites nest in
the wood.

The farmhouse was the former
home of stonecarver, wood
engraver and typographer Eric Gill
who died in 1940 – look out for
his crucifix on one of the trees.

MAP 1

Aston Rowant, Aston Wood & Cowleaze Wood
Watlington/Stokenchurch

Aston Rowant is signposted from the Christmas Common road (off the A40). To visit the northern section use the English Nature car park at the end of the 500m (0.25 mile) long lane, which leads off this road. Visitors to the southern section can park in Cowleaze Wood car park.

Aston Rowant (SU740973), Aston Wood (SU731966), Cowleaze Wood (SU726955), 231ha (571acres)

The National Trust, English Nature & Forestry Commission

Cowleaze Wood

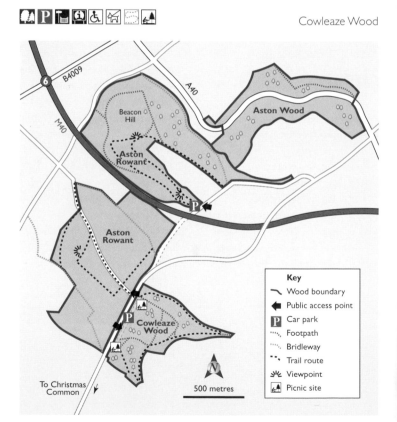

Key

- ⌐ Wood boundary
- ◀ Public access point
- P Car park
- ⋯ Footpath
- ⋯ Bridleway
- ⋯ Trail route
- ☀ Viewpoint
- 🔺 Picnic site

500 metres

MAP 1

Aston Wood

Open landscapes, cooling woodland, wonderful sculptures and countryside views that will take your breath away . . . on a combined visit to these three neighbouring woodlands you can have it all.

Aston Rowant National Nature Reserve, an important chalk downland site on the northwestern scarp of the Chilterns, has some stunning views across the vale of Oxford.

The downland is wonderful and in summer you can see the colourful flowers of Chiltern gentian, wild candytuft, wild thyme, salad burnet plus chalk hill blue and silver spotted skipper butterflies. You can watch red kites, re-introduced to the area in the early 1990s.

Aston Rowant Wood is a great example of a typical Chilterns beechwood. And even though the M40 runs straight through the

Aston Rowant

middle, it's a surprisingly relaxing place to visit.

Well-marked routes aid exploration of the dappled beech woods, where you can enjoy spring carpets of bluebells. Paths north of the road include cherry tree walk, which is suitable for wheelchair and pushchair users, and links to neighbouring Aston Wood.

This mature wood has massive, proud beeches as far as the eye can see. More peaceful than Aston Rowant and its other near neighbour, Cowleaze, it's a spacious and safe open wood with a tranquil, natural feel. There is a lot of ash regeneration in pits which dot the wood.

In contrast, Cowleaze has man's hand on it. Busy and with specially created pathways, it houses the Chilterns Sculpture Trail and children's play facilities.

MAP 1

Hockeridge & Pancake Woods
Berkhamsted & Chesham

Off A41 at A416 towards
Chesham. Right at Ashley Green
(Hog Lane) then right at T Junction
(Johns Lane) past Johns Lane Farm.
Park on roadside layby on right.
(SP978063), 74ha (183acres)

Royal Forestry Society

A riot of colour makes spring
one of the best seasons to visit
this varied site. 52 different species
of hardwood, softwood and
specimen trees can be found on
the ride edges.

While a lot of replanting was
carried out in the 1950s there is a
mixture of ages and species – Scots
pine, spruce, hemlock and larch
along with beech, oak and cherry.

Those interested in its history will
find the information board helpful.
The gnarled hornbeams covering
banks and ditches indicate man's
use of the woods for centuries.
Indeed much of the wood you see
today is on an Iron Age field system
– it was cleared by our ancestors
and replanted afterwards. The mix
of habitats provides homes for
various insects and birds.

There is good access on foot
along the main rides with minor
paths branching off in all kinds
of directions – a compass is
recommended.

Dancersend Nature Reserve
Wendover

On B4009 4km (2.5miles)
northeast of Wendover. Take
unclassified road just south of
A41/B4009 junction, then right at
next T junction. Drive 1.5km
(1 mile) to Thames Waterworks.
Car park on left of main
waterworks building. Cross road to
reserve entrance. (SP905088)
47ha (116acres),
AONB, SSSI

**Berkshire, Buckinghamshire and
Oxfordshire Wildlife Trust**

Beguiling by name, Dancersend
could be 100 miles away from the
bustle of the nearby A41.

The reserve sits in a tranquil
valley and its beautiful mosaic of
meadow, scrub and woodland
creates a mood of calm and
contemplation with views down
across the valley.

A wide range of plants thrive on the chalk grassland – including rare orchids such as the greater butterfly, Chiltern gentian and meadow clary. The sight and smells of common and fragrant basil, thyme and marjoram feed the senses while at the same time sustaining butterflies and moths including the green hairstreak and day-flying burnet moths.

Much-changed since the 1940s when felling took place, the wood is now managed to conserve survivors of the wildwood such as stinking hellebore and the rare yellow bird's nest orchid. Towards the year's end, look out for scarlet elf cup and earth star fungus.

Owners request dogs are kept on a lead at all times.

Dancersend Nature Reserve

MAP 1

Wendover Woodland Park

Wendover
Woodland Park
Wendover

Between Wendover and Tring on
the B4009, take right turn,
north of RAF Halton, signposted
St Leonards and Wendover
Wood. Access 200m on right
(SP887105), 325ha (803acres),
AONB

Forestry Commission

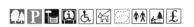

You can enjoy several hours
rambling through the woods,
stopping occasionally to enjoy
views across the Aylesbury valley
and the Chilterns.

Recent extensions to the car

park bear testimony to the popularity of the wood, which provides a variety of routes to meet the needs of hundreds of visitors – from paths and permissive bridleways to a fitness trail, cycle tracks and an orienteering course.

Literally a stone's throw from the car park you can soak up stunning views and appreciate the varied character of the woods, with its mix of beech, ash, oak, birch, Norway maple, spruce, hemlock, larch and Scots pine.

Many conifers have been felled to allow the regeneration of hardwood trees. The site is also managed to encourage nesting, breeding and feeding opportunities for one of its more unusual inhabitants, the scarce firecrest, which lends its name to the circular trail.

Shabbington
Oakley

Take B4011 from Thame to Oakley, turn left into the village and follow minor road round and out of village for 5km (3 miles) towards Horton-cum-Studley. Entrance on left 1.5km (1 mile) after motorway bridge. (SP611117), 287ha (709acres), SSSI

Forestry Commission

Shabbington Wood is one of Britain's most important sites for butterflies and moths – as a summer walk along its butterfly trail will prove.

Home to 40 different species, the wood teems with rare and common butterflies, most notably the black and brown hairstreak, purple emperor, marsh and pearl bordered fritillary and Duke of Burgundy.

The wood once stood at the heart of the ancient forest of Bernwood. Today its fragmented mosaic of woods, pasture meadow and heath is being carefully managed to enhance wildlife habitats and restore native woodland.

During quiet times it is possible to see foxes, muntjac and fallow deer amid the open landscape, peppered with oaks and hazel coppice.

Beyond the wood, the surrounding countryside boasts some of the best open-field systems in Europe and a host of medieval villages.

MAP 1

Piddington Wood
Cherwell
East of Bicester on A41, turn right onto A4011 signed Thame. 1km (0.75 mile) after HM Prison, wood on right. Room for 2-3 cars to park on roadside.
(SP629162), 18ha (44acres)
Woodland Trust

Bats, badgers and butterflies – including the brown hairstreak – feature among the wildlife population thriving on this ancient woodland site, and things are getting better here with the planting of new trees to buffer this precious remnant of the ancient Bernwood hunting forest of Henry ll's reign.

Surrounded by pastureland, the woodland of oak and ash with field maple and hazel was formerly managed by coppicing.

Today the wood is edged with blackthorn with its show of creamy flowers in spring and clusters of purple sloes each autumn.

Set on clay, the path is prone to muddiness in wet seasons, when stout boots or Wellingtons are recommended. The public footpath which leads through the wood forms part of the district council's Piddington circular walk.

Rushbeds Wood
Bicester
5km (3 miles) south of A41 and 11km (7 miles) southeast of Bicester. Turn off A41 at Kingswood on minor road to Boarstall - Wotton Underwood. After 3km (2 miles) just before T junction, car park on right through gate and over railway bridge.
(SP668157)
59ha (143acres), SSSI
Berkshire, Buckinghamshire and Oxfordshire Wildlife Trust

The wildwood is returning to Rushbeds, an ancient woodland site in the Royal Forest of Bernwood, itself a mosaic of pasture, scrub, wetland and woods. Although most of the trees were felled during the 1940s, the site is being allowed to re-establish.

Lying in a wet, fertile valley and surrounded by arable fields and pasture, Rushbeds is a refreshing antidote to the beech woods of the Chilterns. Home to muntjac deer, most of the site is dominated by oak and field maple with willow and aspen in wetter sections.

Rushbeds Wood

Coppicing has been re-introduced in the woodland and butterflies and invertebrates are being encouraged. Spring is a great time to visit when the woods produce an amazing display of bluebells, primroses and moschatel. In summer the meadows are transformed with a sea of oxeye daisies, knapweeds and grassland butterflies.

Owners ask that dogs are kept on a lead at all times.

MAP 1

Finemere Wood

Finemere Wood
Aylesbury

From Aylesbury take A41
(Bicester). After 1.5km (1 mile)
turn right on minor road to
Quainton and continue through
village for 1.5km (1 mile). Turn left
at T junction on unclassified road
for 1km (0.75 mile) and park in
layby on left, 100m before pylons
and railway bridge. Wood on right
up long track.
(SP720215), 45ha (111acres), SSSI

Berkshire, Buckinghamshire and
Oxfordshire Wildlife Trust

All is not what it seems in
Finemere Wood. This is a pine
plantation (only 11ha of planted
pines, the rest is broadleaved and
grassland), fairly remote and you
have a 500m walk to get into
the reserve.

But once inside it reveals itself as a woodland in the throes of change with habitats, scenery – and surprises galore. Goldcrest, bullfinches, kestrel and buzzards are some of the wildlife riches to be found.

You're quickly drawn into the heart of the wood, where scattered, tall oaks offer a feast for woodpeckers and warblers as well as purple hairstreak and white admiral butterflies in their canopy. Look too for trees which are multi-stemmed at their base – evidence of being formerly coppiced.

At its core is an area of rough pasture where many original plant species survive and grazing has been reintroduced to encourage a greater variety of wildlife.

Many small, winding paths provide different perspectives on the woodland. Look out for wild service trees on the uphill section.

Owners request that dogs are kept on a lead at all times.

Stoke Wood
Bicester

Junction 10 off M40, signed Cherwell Services. After services roundabout, head 800m (0.5 mile) north on A43 and then right on B4100 toward Bicester. After 1.5km (1 mile), follow brown sign on left down track to car park. (SP554277), 36ha (89acres)
Woodland Trust

Set in the midst of an otherwise flat landscape, Stoke Wood, just four miles northwest of Bicester, is something of a local landmark, visible from all directions.

This is an ancient woodland site, once managed as hazel coppice with oak standards, though around half of the site was planted in the 1950s with a conifer-broadleaf mixture. The exotic conifers are being phased out, enabling the wood to return to its original character.

Contrasting attractively are several open glades and a small meadow which provide important habitats for invertebrates. More interest comes from the bluebells, primroses and orchids which can be found in the wood along with adder's tongue on the edge of the central ride.

Other features include a large dead cherry, still standing, and a wild service tree. A hornbeam coppice, thought to be ancient, is also worth hunting out.

The tawny owl is resident here.

MAP 1

Stratfield Brake
Kidlington

Turn off A34 at Pear Tree roundabout. Follow A44 towards Woodstock then almost immediately right at next roundabout towards Kidlington. Just before dual carriageway ends turn left into Stratfield Brake sports ground.
(SP492120), 19ha (47acres)
Woodland Trust

A small area of mature woodland at the southern edge of Stratfield Brake is in the early stages of an interesting evolution that will benefit nature and mankind alike.

Here is woodland in the making.

A large swathe of young trees, planted ten years ago, is now emerging. This adjoins open ground which is grazed, a large wetland project created in partnership with the Environment Agency and a new sports field.

The Woodland Trust, presented with the land by Oxfordshire County Council, is transforming another area of bare land, farmed until recently, into yet more woodland as part of its Tree for All campaign.

The new wood will provide a screen to the busy dual carriageway alongside. Its future popularity as a recreation facility looks almost certain.

Foxholes Wood
Chipping Norton

From A424 take road to Bruern Abbey, 500m (0.25 mile) past turn to Milton under Wychwood, take rough track to left following edge of wood for 800m (0.5 mile).
(SP252205), 66ha (165acres)
Berkshire. Buckinghamshire and Oxfordshire Wildlife Trust

Allow lots of time to soak up delightful Foxholes Nature Reserve – and then return time and again to get the best of each season.

This large, gently sloping site – once part of the ancient Wychwood Forest – has a choice of four marked routes to explore.

In spring you are greeted by the bright displays of pink campions, primroses, violets, bugle and early purple orchids and from March to April you might spot speckled wood butterflies or hear the croaky male woodcock. In May the wood is awash with bluebells.

Return in June to enjoy majestic foxgloves and yellow-green herb-paris while meadow brown, comma, large and small and green-veined white and white admiral butterflies flourish.

Autumn colours are complemented by more than 200 fungi species while in winter, when you might get a glimpse of muntjac, roe and fallow deer, frost on the leaves adds a magical feeling.

Barton Hills
Barton Le Clay
Off A6, 9.5 km (6 miles) north of Luton from village take B655. Barton Le Clay accessed via Church Road Barton off B655. Park by church.
(TL088297), 40ha (99acres), SSSI
English Nature

Your visit is promptly rewarded by impressive views of a steep-sided chalk valley with woodland on the western side and extensive areas of nationally important chalk grassland on the remainder.

The wooded side of the valley consists mainly of typical Chilterns beech woodland on dry chalk slopes, and ash and maple on the damp soils alongside a clear chalk stream in the valley bottom. The wood includes typical plants such as bluebell, wood anemone, yellow archangel and dog violet. There are also some less common plants such as white helleborine, herb paris, stinking iris and spurge laurel.

The chalk grassland is notable for its rare plants – fleawort and pasque flower among them – and rare invertebrates, as well as a mix of species that are characteristic of the Chilterns, for example clustered bellflower and small skipper butterfly.

There are short circular walks within the site but for those more adventurous a brisk climb of the downs provides panoramic views, including the neighbouring earthworks of Ravensburgh Castle. From here the play of light on downland, meadow and woods is exquisite.

47

MAP 2

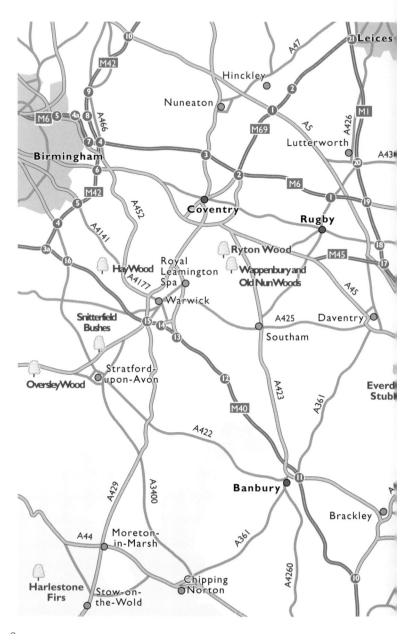

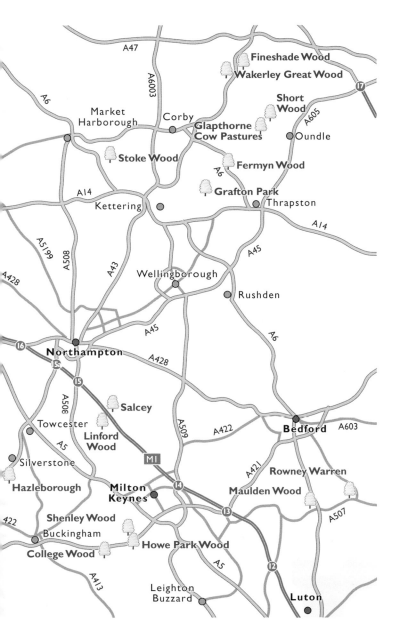

A47

A6003

A6

Market Harborough

Corby

Fineshade Wood

Wakerley Great Wood

Short Wood

A605

Glapthorne Cow Pastures

Oundle

Stoke Wood

Fermyn Wood

A6

Grafton Park

A14

Kettering

Thrapston

A14

A5199

A508

A43

Wellingborough

A45

A428

Rushden

A45

A6

16

Northampton

15a

A428

15

A508

Salcey

Towcester

Linford Wood

A5

Silverstone

M1

A509

A422

Bedford

A603

Hazleborough

A421

Rowney Warren

Milton Keynes

14

Maulden Wood

A507

13

422

Shenley Wood

Buckingham

Howe Park Wood

College Wood

12

A5

A413

Leighton Buzzard

Luton

MAP 2

Maulden Wood
Clophill

Wood accessed from the
Deadman's Hill layby on
A6 northbound, 1.5km (1 mile)
from Clophill (TL073395)
183ha (452acres), SSSI
Forestry Commission

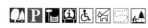

Sited atop the gently undulating
terrain of the Greensand ridge,
Maulden is one of Bedfordshire's
largest ancient woodland sites.

Spring brings masses of bluebells
and wood sorrel. Summer finds it
full of birds and butterflies, and a
succession of colourful wild
flowers, including orchids. In
autumn it is a great place to come
to watch the subtly changing
colours of the many different
kinds of tree.

Well-surfaced trails provide a
good choice of rambles, and the
throb of the nearby A6 is soon
forgotten as you meander through
mature oak, ash and beech with
hazel and hornbeam coppice.

Wetter sections feature aspen,
willow and elm, with summer
swathes of meadowsweet lining
the ditches, ponds and streams
interspersed with dense
compartments of birch, ash, hazel,
dogwood and field maple.

There are Scots pine, larch and
spruce – all in various stages of
thinning. At the ride edges,
chestnut, red oak, Norway maple
and cherry create a more
ornamental feel.

Rowney Warren
Shefford

On A600 3km (2 miles) north of
Shefford. Car park accessed from
Sandy Lane.
(TL124404), 71ha (175acres)
Forestry Commission

The origins of this interesting site's
name date back to medieval times
when it was enclosed for the
farming of rabbits.

Today, the mainly coniferous
woodland shelters a variety of
creatures, among them foxes,
voles, mice, lizards, grass snakes –
and humans.

A maze of minor tracks leading
off a well-maintained central ride
network makes this a great site
for walkers and cyclists,
particularly in the northern
section where the terrain is a
little more challenging.

As well as crossbills and siskins feeding off the pine cones, Rowney Warren is a favourite nesting site for buzzards and sparrow hawks. On hot summer evenings there is also the chance of spotting glow-worms at the southern edge of the wood.

Much of the site was planted with Scots and Corsican pine, and larch between the 1930s-50s. Now, as many sections reach maturity and are felled, clearings are being created in preparation for an anticipated re-growth of acid heathland. Heather has been seeded in some areas, and there are signs of a tentative comeback.

Shenley Wood
Milton Keynes

Turn off A421 north onto Tattenhoe Street V2. Go across Oxley Park roundabout and next left into Merlewood Drive. Car park signposted on left. (SP825357), 23ha (57acres)

The Parks Trust, Milton Keynes

Shenley Wood is a well-loved urban woodland with a rural feel that sits in the heart of Berkshire, Buckinghamshire and Oxfordshire's butterfly 'capital' – Milton Keynes.

Despite its popularity with locals and a year-round events programme, Shenley – Saxon for 'bright clearing' – has an intimate feel. Visitors can enjoy easy walking and cycling through this semi-natural ancient woodland.

The woodland boasts 160 different species of plants. Spring produces a wonderful show of bluebells, primroses and wood anemones as well as the relatively rare pale sedge, everlasting pea and greater butterfly orchid.

The entrances are inviting and lead the visitor along a subtly changing network of gravel and woodchip paths, and wide, flower-edged grassy rides which, not surprisingly, attract large numbers and types of butterfly and moth.

The paths lead through a mixture of oak and ash high forest with a hazel and field maple understorey. Other shrubs include thorns, goat willow, dogwood, guelder rose, purging buckthorn and wayfaring tree.

MAP 2

Howe Park Wood
Milton Keynes

Turn off A421 (Standing Way H8)
into Snelshall Street V1 towards
Tattenhoe and Westcroft. Turn right
at Kingsmead roundabout into
Chaffron Way H7. Car park signed
off road opposite to Westcroft
shopping area. (SP831345)
23ha (57acres), SSSI
The Parks Trust, Milton Keynes

Nestling next to a 21st-century
shopping precinct in the southwest
of Milton Keynes, this beautifully
preserved wood is the area's jewel
in its woodland crown.

Featured in the Domesday survey
as an ancient woodland park,
Howe Park nurtures bluebells and
orchids in spring and butterflies in
late summer. Informal seating in
the glades allows you to sit and
enjoy the wildlife which, as the
evening falls, can witness
appearances by muntjac, fox,
badger or bats.

This special site is full of
character, crossed by paths that
twist and turn through a changing

Howe Park Wood

landscape of oak, ash, aspen and maple, with thorn thickets, dogwood, field maple and ancient crab apples.

Oak and ash dominate the main woodland where careful management has opened up pockets of light and shade, allowing plants and insects to thrive or migrate with ease.

While wet and heavy soils have helped the wood survive intact, stout shoes are recommended in all but the driest of conditions.

College Wood
Nash, Milton Keynes

Turn north off A421 between Buckingham and Milton Keynes, signed Wood End. Wood and car park on right. (SP791330), 52ha (128acres)
Woodland Trust

Muntjac deer, rabbits and badgers feature among the wildlife population in this ancient coppice woodland, which sits on the lip of a plateau.

Historically part of the Whaddon chasehunting forest, College Wood was once divided into three coppices by ditch and bank and surrounded by common pasture.

Extensive felling in the 1950s and 60s saw vigorous planting – of spruce, larch, cypress, oak, beech and Scots pine.

A natural cover of ash, oak and field maple and remnants of hawthorn, hazel, sallow and bramble still survive, along with a bluebell-dominated woodland floor where early purple orchid and wood anemone add interest.

Once designated of special scientific interest for its invertebrate population, the site was denotified after extensive felling and replanting. But, with the Woodland Trust's help, there are signs that wood white and white admiral butterflies are back again, visiting the woodland rides.

Hazleborough
Silverstone

From Silverstone village take minor road west signposted Abthorpe, keeping straight on towards A43 slip road but turning right into wood across junction. (SP660431), 407ha (1006acres)
Forestry Commission ▸▸

MAP 2

Thanks to extensive paths and rides, visitors can find quiet corners in this ancient woodland where peace is enjoyed. Follow the waymarked trail for a real feel of the ancient oak woods with their understorey of hazel and thorns. Look out too for ash, field maple, willow and dogwood.

Springtime visits will be rewarded with a knockout performance of birdsong and a stunning display of heady-smelling bluebells. In fact, this must be one of the region's best bluebell sites, with virtually the whole western side carpeted in swathes of their distinctive blue and green hues.

Early butterflies flit across the rides and roe and fallow deer can be sighted. At dusk, keep an eye out for badgers along with noctule and long-eared bats.

Linford Wood
Milton Keynes

North on B526 from Newton Pagnell, after 3km (2 miles) take road on left to Haversham; after 750m (0.5 mile) take private track on right signposted Dairy Farm, and continue for 1.5km (1 mile) under M1 and past farm. (SP834455), 43ha (106acres)

Berkshire, Buckinghamshire & Oxfordshire Wildlife Trust

Here is a relatively young wood that feels like ancient woodland.

It is home to an array of plants and animals including stoats, kestrels, buzzards and foxes, probably accounting for the 'aged' feel of the wood, which is crisscrossed with footpaths and bridleways. A third of the site was felled by a previous owner in the 1980s resulting in the present-day mix of old and young trees.

A good bet is to follow the wildlife walk signs into the woodland where oak and ash are regenerating vigorously.

The dense shrub layer has been coppiced regularly, opening up areas for flowering plants, insects and mammals, including dormice, which were reintroduced in 1998.

The rides lead down to wildwood remnants where you can find primrose, cuckoo flower, bluebell and ragged robin in spring. Spreading oak and ash are dotted with clusters of elm, crab apple and dogwood.

Owner requests dogs are kept on a lead at all times.

Salcey Forest
Hartwell Village

Just off B526 from Newport Pagnell. Located between Quinton and Hanslop. Follow brown tourist signs.
(SP795515), 510ha (1261 acres), SSSI

Forestry Commission

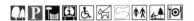

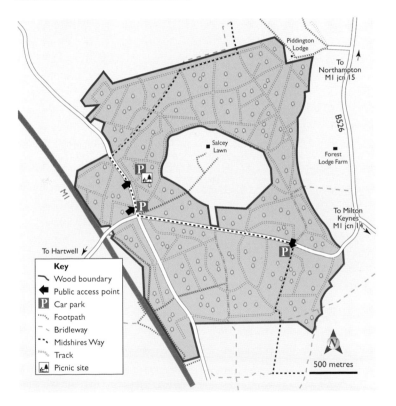

Lime Avenue, Salcey Forest   Veteran Oak, Salcey Forest

From rich wildlife and beautiful woodland walks to visitor facilities and special events, cycle trails and a few surprises to keep you on your toes – Salcey Forest has it all.

It's the largest area of open-access woodland for a considerable distance, has a rich history and still provides an important timber resource.

This diverse and delightful site is set right alongside the M1, though the traffic rumble quickly fades. And even though hundreds of visitors flock here daily, only around the visitor centre does it become crowded.

At its heart lies the English oak, grown from the early 18th century to augment hazel coppice and provide timber for ship construction.

As you explore the forest you encounter a number of 'druid oaks' and quaintly named pollards – such as Piddington and Milking Oak – which provide homes for rare and specialised lichen, invertebrates and fungi.

Earthen wood banks define hazel coppices that surround pasture land which suggests that, unusually, the site is more wooded today than in the past.

Rich in wildlife, the site is noted for butterflies – among them wood white, brown argus, black hairstreak, grizzled and dingy skipper and clouded yellow. Primroses, bluebells, arum and wild garlic add seasonal colour.

To get a feel for the forest, take any one of three waymarked trails. Elephant Walk gives easy access – and a view of a pond that was used to cool off elephants as they extracted timber during World War Two – while Church Path takes in a fallen veteran oak and Woodpecker Trail circles the whole site. Plans for a new aerial walkway are bound to bring an added dimension to your woodland visit.

MAP 2

Everdon Stubbs
Daventry

Leave Daventry on A45 towards Northampton. After 5km (3 miles), in village of Dodford, turn right towards Everdon. At T junction turn left. Small car park on side of road as it goes through the wood. (SP606566), 29ha (82acres), SSSI
Woodland Trust

Unusually for the East Midlands, Everdon Stubbs is an ancient woodland made up of differing woodland communities. There are, in fact, two separate woods – Everdon Stubbs and Everdon Wood.

Containing an unusual mix of common and sessile oak with lowland birch growing on top of the ridge, both woods also have sections of sweet chestnut and sycamore.

There is an abundance of spring colour provided both by bluebells and the county's largest population of rare wild daffodils. Other locally rare plants include moschatel, broom, gorse and wild raspberry.

Historians will be interested to know the site has been documented since the 10th century and its believed part of a prehistoric burial site remains on its northern boundary.

Everdon Stubbs

Harlestone Firs
Northampton

Follow A428 from Northampton towards Rugby. Harlestone Firs is approx 500m (0.5 mile) from Northampton on right, opposite garden centre
(SP119294)

The Althorp Estate

Prized for its impressive array of fungi and home to colonies of wood ants, Harlestone Firs is also popular with walkers and riders.

Close to the village of Harlestone, it provides a buffer between town and countryside and forms a key landscape feature on the outskirts of Northampton.

Sitting on a sandy ridge, this was once heathland, a scarce resource in the county today, as is evident from clearings in the wood where dwarf gorse is colonising areas of acid grassland.

The wood is dominated by Scots pine with some larch although a few mature Douglas firs can be found.

Harlestone Firs

MAP 2

Stoke Wood

Stoke Wood
Stoke Albany

If approaching from west turn off A427 north into Stoke Albany. From the east turn north into Wilbarston and continue to Stoke Albany. Turn left signed Market Harborough, under A427 and approx 1.5km (1 mile) out of village, park in small layby on left by private wood. Follow track across fields on opposite side of road into wood.
(SP800863), 11ha (27acres)
Woodland Trust

Stoke Wood was regularly coppiced until as recently as 1970 and dominated today by ash trees. Field maple, oaks and small areas of birch rise above hazel, dogwood, spindle, blackthorn, dog rose and willow.

The unusually diverse mix of ground flora found in this relatively small wood includes floral displays of bluebells as well as herb paris, wood anemone, wood sorrel, yellow archangel, early purple orchid, wood speedwell and nettle-leaved bell flower.

The scenery changes regularly, with high forest and some neglected coppice in the northern sections compared to active coppice and standards in the heart of the wood, much of it thanks to a group of enthusiastic volunteers.

Grafton Park

Grafton Park
Kettering

From A43, 13km (8 miles) north of Kettering, turn into village of Geddington (tourist sign to Boughton House). Following minor road to Grafton Underwood, turn left at T junction. Wood entrance on right after 1km (0.5 mile) (SP928815), 116ha (287acres)
Broughton Estates Ltd

Not many woods boast a roundabout at their heart that was home to a World War Two cinema. Grafton Park does.

Its fascinating history, including being part of a 14th-century hunting forest, can be discovered on a walk through this accessible, welcoming and tranquil woodland.

Evidence of air raid shelters and barracks evoke wartime activity when this was a US bomber crew base.

The site's ancient origins can be seen in landmarks such as earthen boundary banks and the rich ground flora, dominated in spring by dog's mercury, bluebells and primroses.

The main trees here are oak and ash with a scattering of birch but there are also some beech, sycamore and hornbeam.

At the centre, eight paths radiate out providing a variety of alternative routes, though not all are open.

MAP 2

Fermyn Woods
Corby

Take the A43 Kettering to Corby road to Stanion and join the A6116 heading southeast for about 6.5km (4 miles). Entrance to Fermyn Woods via country park on left. Look for brown tourist sign. Follow trail into woodland from park.
(SP955850), 506ha (1250acres)
Forestry Commission

Well-used by walkers, Fermyn is an all-season, accessible treasure trove of plants, animals, birds and butterflies.

  The Forestry Commission is managing the site to encourage traditional broadleaves to flourish, as conifer crops of pine and

Fermyn Woods

spruce are gradually removed on reaching maturity.

Summer is a good time to see reptiles such as the common lizard basking in the sun, while autumn brings many different types of fungi.

The site is particularly favoured by birdwatchers. Little owls, nightingales and crossbills have been spotted here. Rockingham Forest is also known for its red kites and other birds of prey.

Despite its popularity, it is easy to get away along quiet paths to enjoy the qualities of this ancient woodland site.

The openness of the rides lends a secure feeling, making this an ideal destination for families, who can make use of the country park facilities as well as exploring the open glades, ponds and wetland areas.

Glapthorn Cow Pastures
Oundle

Access from the road between Glapthorn and Benefield, about 1.5km (1 mile) from Glapthorn. Park on the broad verge of the lane south of the road. (TL005903), 28ha (69acres), SSSI

The Wildlife Trust for Bedfordshire, Cambridgeshire, Northamptonshire & Peterborough

A maze of quiet roads in a gently rolling landscape paves the way for a very special kind of rural retreat that literally assaults the senses.

This ash–maple woodland features oak specimen trees, occasionally left to fall and decompose, thereby providing sculpted homes for a mass of insects, birds, mosses, fungi and lichen.

A circular walk lets you appreciate the many aspects of the wood – from dense shrub and understorey through extensive glades into high ash forest with signs of ridge and furrow beneath, while a bridleway at the northeastern corner leads to Short Wood (see next entry), providing views across the valley.

It supports a variety of species, including breeding nightingale, warblers and woodcock. Open rides and specimen trees favour the uncommon black hairstreak butterfly.

Spring flora includes primroses, bluebells, orchids, common centaury, bugle and yellow archangel.

MAP 2

Short Wood
Oundle

Turn at stone memorial in Oundle centre towards Southwick. After Glapthorn village, park in layby at top of hill on left before water tower. A signpost just before layby directs you a field length along track to wood.
(TL015913), 26ha (62acres)

The Wildlife Trust for Bedfordshire, Cambridgeshire, Northamptonshire & Peterborough

Said to be the finest bluebell wood in the whole of Northamptonshire – a legacy of its ancient woodland origins – this is, in fact, four distinct woods.

Short Wood and Dodhouse Wood lie on the north side, with Hall Wood and Rockshaft Close to the south.

The reserve is a mix of primary and old secondary woodland with ash and field maple supplemented by oak with sections of hazel coppice. In Short Wood, look for coppiced elms – a type found only in the East Midlands and probably the oldest example known. It is clinging on to life, post-Dutch elm disease.

The site's remoteness allows, on quiet mornings or at dusk, the chance to listen to foraging animals, bats, birdsong and predators seeking out food.

The birdlife population includes three woodpecker species, tawny owl, marsh and willow warbler and tree creeper.

Fineshade Wood
Corby

Off the A43 Corby to Stamford road 3 km (2 miles) from the junction with the A47 Peterborough/Leicester junction. Follow brown tourist sign at crossroads for Wakerley Wood but turn the opposite direction down a narrow lane running east. Car park is up the hill.
(SP979984), 311ha (768acres)
Forestry Commission

Steeped in cultural heritage and renowned for its wildlife and recreation opportunities, Fineshade Wood is being managed to gradually restore its ancient woodland character.

A great place for families, cyclists, bird-watchers and natural history enthusiasts alike, the woodland lies in the heart of Rockingham Forest and still shows signs of its medieval history and royal hunting forest heritage.

Bustling with life, particularly at weekends, the site has a busy programme of activities including badger and kite-watching.

You can discover remnants of the ancient woodland cover amongst scattered spruce and pine – evidence of previous conifer plantation.

There is an opportunity to enjoy good views across the valley to Wakerley and beyond.

Wakerley Great Wood
Corby

Follow A43 from Corby for approximately 15km (9.5 miles). Before village of Duddington, follow brown tourist sign at crossroads to left. Car park 500m on left through main entrance. (SP955975), 261ha (640acres), SSSI

Forestry Commission

This ancient woodland site is second only to Bedford Purlieus as Rockingham Forest's best fungi site and its geology has produced some unexpected plants.

Rare trees, such as small-leaved lime and wild service survive in the wood, along with other echoes of its past – a veteran beech tree near the ironstone quarries and former charcoal production sites. The area is rich in archaeology dating back to the Bronze Age.

A mix of broadleaves and conifers, its ancient woodland character is being restored and evidence of its origins become apparent on a tour. Take care in shady areas, where it can get muddy underfoot.

The entrance is welcoming, with a mix of mature larch, oak, pine and spruce – swathes of spruce dominated the wood until some 15 years ago. Today few remain and traditional coppicing now takes place in the wood.

Open glades have been extended to encourage invertebrates such as glow-worms. There are six species of orchid and other rare and unusual plants. The wood is home to many butterflies including white admiral, grizzled skipper and numerous others. It is a popular woodland for birdwatchers who come to see the red kites.

Walking, cycling and horse riding are all permitted and the picnic site has barbecue points. There are trails suitable for pushchairs and wheelchair users.

MAP 2

Ryton Wood

Ryton Wood
Leamington Spa

Signed off the A445 via Ryton
Pools Country Park.
(SP370724), 84ha (208acres), SSSI
Warwickshire Wildlife Trust

Dating back to the 11th century,
this large site, a haven for birds and
butterflies, is one of Warwickshire's
largest surviving semi-natural
ancient woodland sites.

The best route in is through
Ryton Pools Country Park, which
boasts lots of facilities including a
visitor centre.

While it's adjacent to a
sometimes-bustling country park,
the wood is large enough to allow
you to escape the crowds.

Designated a site of special
scientific interest, here you'll
discover an interesting mix of oak,
hazel and small-leaved lime with
silver birch, holly, wild strawberry,
lesser celandine, violet,
honeysuckle and primrose.

Observant visitors might identify
some of the 30 species of trees and
shrubs, 80 species of bird and 33
of butterfly that are present.

Man, too, is free to roam an
extensive ride system radiating out
from the centre of the reserve,
with its marshy areas, ponds and
open glades.

Wappenbury & Old Nun woods
Leamington Spa

At the roundabout where the A445 meets the A423, head south west on A423. Turn right at Princethorpe on B4453, and take right into Burnthurst Lane through woods. Park by the bend on Burnthurst Lane and walk down track to reach the woods. (SP380709), 74ha (181acres)

Warwickshire Wildlife Trust

A visit to Wappenbury Woods can be easily combined with its small but interesting neighbour Old Nun Wood, which is well worth a short stroll en route to the larger wood.

Both Old Nun and Wappenbury woods were felled in the 1940s but have since been left to regenerate. Their origins are ancient, with Wappenbury being mentioned in the Domesday Book.

Old Nun Wood has a circular walk which leads visitors along a path edged with bluebells, yellow archangel, wood sorrel and wood anemone. Today its birdlife includes the garden warbler, chiffchaff, tree creeper, blue tit and great spotted woodpecker.

A short hop across a ditch and you're in Wappenbury. Closed on Wednesdays and Saturdays, coppicing management has been re-introduced to create greater interest in this oak, ash and small-leaved lime woodland. The result is a healthy regeneration of hazel, ash, silver birch and aspen.

The site has spectacular displays of plants on the rides and in the open spaces, and these provide habitats for birds and butterflies such as speckled wood, white admiral, wood white and peacock.

Muntjac, roe and fallow deer and badgers are also resident. In spring the woodland floor is a carpet of flowers and is the best time to visit. The rides have waymarked walks though they can be wet.

MAP 2

Hay Wood
Baddesley Clinton

From A4141 at village of Baddesley Clinton take left towards Baddesley Clinton Manor, then first left down minor road. Wood is on the left.
(SP205707), 105ha (260acres)
Forestry Commission

Popular with dog walkers, Hay Wood is a pleasant conifer plantation on an ancient woodland site, where visitors might spot squirrels, roe and muntjac deer, rabbits and mallards and enjoy glimpses of the surrounding countryside.

There are some deciduous trees on the site and, unusually for a conifer plantation, spring carpets of bluebells under well-spaced conifers.

Other species to look out for include butterflies flitting up and down the wide forest rides, pines, holly and silver birch. Two waymarked routes are easy to follow and range from one to two miles, taking the visitor along level and mainly wide forest tracks, though some are rutted and muddy.

Snitterfield Bushes
Stratford upon Avon

From A46 turn into village of Snitterfield, and follow minor Snitterfield to Bearley road. Heading west, car park on left at beginning of wood, entrance on right.
(SP200603), 120ha (300acres), SSSI
Warwickshire Wildlife Trust

Brimming with birdsong and blanketed with a delightful spread

Snitterfield Bushes

of rare woodland plants including early purple orchid and primroses, Snitterfield Bushes is a well-tended woodland where deer and butterflies thrive.

The nature reserve is all that remains of a much larger broadleaved woodland of ash, oak and silver birch that once stretched to Bearley. But that changed in 1910 when a wartime airfield was built, though the network of concrete tracks left behind provides an excellent network of dry tracks through quite a wet woodland.

Evidence of ridge and furrow indicates the area was once cultivated.

The rich, damp clay soil is overlain by mossy banks of bluebells, figwort, violets, herb paris and coltsfoot. Some wayfaring trees and midland hawthorn are present.

Look out too for white admiral, purple hairstreak, and marbled white butterflies.

Oversley Wood
Alcester
From A46 take minor road to Alcester and Aldersley Green, after 350m (0.25 mile) turn into unmarked track on left, which passes back under the A46. (SP110566), 93ha (230acres)
Forestry Commission

It takes just a little while to escape the thunder of traffic sounds from the nearby A46 as you venture into the heart of Oversley Wood.

The woodland's diverse mixture of silver birch, oak and conifers act as an effective sound buffer.

The main forest track makes for easy walking through this ancient woodland site, while smaller paths have a tendency to be muddy.

Once inside, ranks of old oaks are enjoying more space and light with the removal of competing conifers and appear to have been given a new lease of life.

In spring you can find glades of bluebells, the occasional cluster of primroses and wild cherry blossom adding a pretty garnish to the forest track edges. In early summer the track edges become a haze of orchids.

Visitors with limited mobility can ring ahead for an access code to enter the woods via a locked gate. See 'Useful Contacts' on p129.

MAP 3

A483
A5
A53
A442
A458 **Shrewsbury**
Haughmond Hill
Telf
A5
7 6
Welshpool
A488
The Ercall
Severn Gorge
Coalbrookd
Much Wenlock
Wenlock Edge
Workhous
Coppice
A490
A489
Church
Stretton
A49
Helmeth Hill
A458
Bridgnort
Bishop's
Castle
A488
Bury Ditches
Clun
Hopton Wood
A4113
Ludlow
A4117
A488
Knighton
Mortimer Forest
A456
Croft
Woodlands
A49
A4112
A410
Leominster
A44
Kington
Easters Wood
A44
A4112
A417
Bromyard
Brockhan
A4111
A460
A438
A465
A410

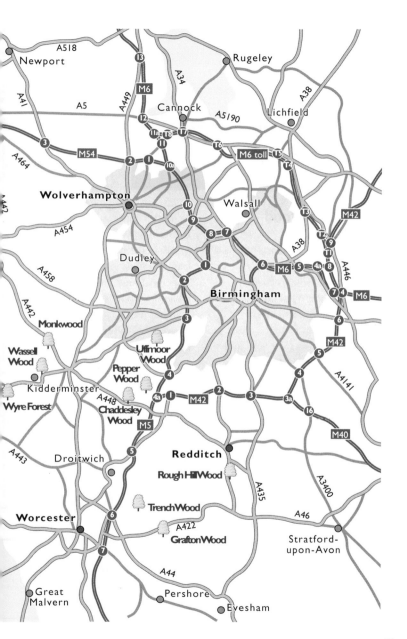

71

MAP 3

Rough Hill Wood

Rough Hill Wood
Redditch

Take the A448 southeast. Where it meets the A441, just south of Redditch, the wood is located adjacent to the A448 on left. Access via the surrounding housing estates.
(SP052637), 21ha (52acres), SSSI
Warwickshire Wildlife Trust

Providing a breath of air for the residents of a modern housing estate that totally surrounds it, Rough Hill Wood has its roots firmly in the past, dating back at least 400 years.

Species found on the site, including wood sorrel, crab apple, wild service tree, midland hawthorn, small-leaved lime and pendulous sedge, affirm its ancient origins and the site has been designated of special scientific interest.

Divided into six distinct compartments, this wood is well used and loved by local residents.

Grafton Wood
Grafton Flyford

From A422 take turning to Grafton Flyford. Take first right signposted to village hall. Park in front of church and follow footpath eastwards across fields to wood.
(SO962557), 56ha (138acres), SSSI

Worcestershire Wildlife Trust & Butterfly Conservation Society

Set in quintessential English countryside, history–steeped Grafton Wood is home to the last remaining Midlands colony of the rare brown hairstreak butterfly.

This ancient site actually sustains no fewer than 26 species of butterfly along with fabulously named woodland flora such as adders' tongue fern, bird's nest orchid, saw-wort and herb Paris.

A semi-natural broadleaved woodland, the site boasts oak, ash, aspen and birch among a host of other species. Huge ancient pollarded oak and ash are living evidence of the great age of this wood.

Venturing further, a circle of small-leaved lime coppice probably dates back 1,000 years. In fact, the wood was managed for centuries as coppice and the same system is now being reintroduced, creating glades and wide rides – great for butterflies.

An extensive network of paths offer lots of opportunities for exploration across gently undulating ground, though boots are recommended since it can get muddy.

Trench Wood
Worcester

From A4538 1.5km (1 mile) south of junction 6 on M5 take turning off roundabout to Crowle Green. Go through village and fork left to Sale Green and then left at T junction. Car park on left on the edge of wood.
(SO928590), 42ha (103acres), SSSI
Worcesterershire Wildlife Trust

A delight to explore, that's Trench Wood; a lovely ancient woodland that was managed until the 1960s as coppice.

The site features birch and oak with areas of hazel beneath and some semi-mature sycamore.

As part of Worcestershire Wildlife

Trust's efforts to improve the wildlife habitat value of the site, some sections are managed as scrub. Not only does this support migrant summer warblers such as blackcap, garden warbler, chiff chaff and willow warbler, it also enriches the experience of visitors by creating open, sunnier areas.

From here you can observe butterflies such as white admirals, skippers, ringlets, gatekeepers and peacocks.

There are many wildflowers too – among them herb Paris – a species indicating ancient woodland status – and greater butterfly orchid.

It is worth noting that two sections are privately owned so visitors should take care not to wander in.

MAP 3

Chaddesley Wood
Bromsgrove

From A448, 5km (3 miles) west of Bromsgrove, turn into Woodcote Lane signposted Dordale and Belbroughton. Take left fork along Woodcote Green Lane. Wood lies to either side of road.
(SO915736), 101ha (250acres), SSSI
Worcestershire Wildlife Trust

Popular with locals, Chaddesley Wood is a rich, delightful ancient-woodland site with wonderful views across the rolling Worcestershire countryside.

Parts are believed to have remained wooded for up to 10,000 years. Once part of the royal hunting Forest of Feckenham, this may be the 'wood of the two leagues' from the Domesday Book.

Today it is a mosaic of coniferous plantation and semi-natural woodland, split by a minor road. This variety makes it a delight, with undulating rides, a choice of routes, good waymarking and constant birdsong. It is also home to the nationally rare terrestrial caddis insect.

The western coniferous section is managed as a valuable habitat for summer migrants such as warblers and blackcaps.

The eastern section is dominated by oak, including former hazel coppice and species-rich pasture, which is a site of special scientific interest. A short footpath along its southern boundary is worth exploring.

Chaddesley Wood

Pepper Wood

Pepper Wood
Fairfield, Bromsgrove

Following the B4091 south, turn right at mini-roundabout into Pepper Wood Road. Turn right at end into Dordale Road. Wood and car park 400 metres (0.25 mile) on right.
(SO937749), 54ha (133acres), SSSI
Woodland Trust

Pepper Wood is a remnant of the historic Forest of Feckenham, dating back to the 13th century.

Dominated by oak and birch, the wood boasts an exceptional diversity of tree and shrub species – small and large-leaved lime and wild service are all to be found here.

There are several less common and some rare species recorded in the wood, from thick spiked wood sedge and broad and violet hellebore to white admiral butterfly and a variety of moths. A small pond adds to the wood's interest.

The site is easy to access and popular with locals. A good network of rides gives visitors the chance to explore areas of coppice, high forest and quiet narrow paths.

MAP 3

Uffmoor Wood
Halesowen

Following A456 south of
Halesowen, turn left up Uffmoor
Lane. Parking and main wood
entrance located 400m (0.25 mile)
on left.
(SO952811), 85ha (210acres)
Woodland Trust

Stretching across gently sloping land,
Uffmoor Wood is an important
friend to the urban visitor, being just
a mile outside of Halesowen.

Popular despite its isolation – the
site is surrounded by pasture – the
wood is easily accessed thanks to a
public footpath network and an
excellent web of rides including
three waymarked routes.

Most of the site is planted ancient
woodland, dominated by stands of
conifers and mixed broadleaves
with birch regeneration. A few
isolated pockets of semi-natural
ancient woodland can still be
found, along the edges of
watercourses.

Regular coppicing in the past has
created a distinct woodland
structure, still evident in the
southeast corner though most of the
site is now dominated by plantation.

Ground flora is varied and
interesting, including several species
which point to its ancient
woodland origins.

Uffmoor Wood

Monkwood
Worcester

Turning off A443 onto minor road signposted Sinton Green and Wichenford, follow brown signs. (SO804806), 61ha (151acres), SSSI
Worcestershire Wildlife Trust and Butterfly Conservation Society

History merges with nature in Monkwood. For this is an ancient woodland site, surrounded by earth banks and brimming with wildlife – including 36 different butterfly species.

Felled in the 1970s and replanted with a broadleaf-conifer mix, the wood has hung onto much of its ancient woodland character.

Bisected by a minor road, it features a particularly diverse northern section where woodland pools provide a habitat for dragonflies. In spring comes a sea of bluebells and wood anemones and, in autumn, fungi are abundant and fallen crab apples add colour to the woodland floor.

Wassell Wood
Trimpley

Follow B4190 southeast of Kidderminster. Turn right before Catchems End into Trimpley Lane and right at fork up Hoarstone Lane. Wood 800m on right. (SO795774), 22ha (54acres)
Woodland Trust

A prominent feature of the area, cloaking a steep hill overlooking Kidderminster, Bewdley and the Severn valley.

Sitting atop the level summit is the site of a scheduled ancient monument from where you can enjoy views of the surrounding countryside.

The hill's lower eastern slopes have been heavily thinned in the past and are now seeing birch and sycamore regenerate together with regrowth of oak and sweet chestnut coppice.

The rest of the site, believed to be a remnant of early 20th century planting, is a mature mixture of oak, ash and sycamore.

Well used by walkers and riders, the site has a helpful network of paths and bridleways.

MAP 3

Wyre Forest
Kidderminster

Wyre Forest is well signed from the A456.
(SO750739), 1052ha (2598acres), SSSI

Forestry Commission

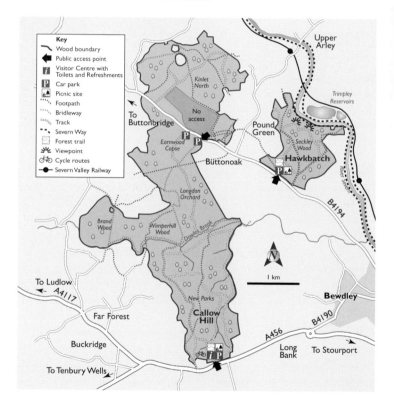

Wyre Forest

This vast, dense forest – so massive it dominates the landscape – is a real family draw with 2,500 acres to explore, offering something for all the family.

The site is all that survives of an historic wild wood which, centuries ago, stretched along the Severn valley from Worcester to Bridgnorth and much of what remains has now been designated of special scientific interest.

There are lots of facilities – including a shop, schools' discovery centre, café and children's play area – and a comprehensive events calendar. The rambling forest itself is thickly clad in conifers, with an ancient oak woodland – a national nature reserve – at its heart.

The best way to explore is probably by bicycle, thanks to many well-marked and well-surfaced cycle routes. There are three waymarked trails, ranging from 1.4km to a family cycling route of 5.3km and a 7.7km family mountain-bike route. The more adventurous can venture deeper into the forest for miles on more challenging tracks in an area known as Kinlet North.

En route, you might encounter fallow deer, tree creepers, hornets and brown hawker moths and spot wood ants, parasol mushrooms, bilberries, orchids or even a wild service tree.

This is a working forest, that still generates a large amount of timber annually.

MAP 3

Haughmond Hill

Haughmond Hill
Shrewsbury

Take the B5062 Shrewsbury to
Newport road, turn right after
Haughmond Abbey. Past the
quarry entrance, car park on right.
(SJ546148), 132ha (326acres)
Forestry Commission

Perched on Haughmond Hill,
overlooking a vast landscape,
this forest is a mix of Scots and
Corsican pine, trees that enjoy
the heath-like conditions of
the hill.

Shrewsbury is close by and
consequently the woodland is well
used, yet it is surprisingly peaceful
with just intermittent signs and
sounds of its many visitors.

The conifer planting is quite
dense in places but a well-signed
series of waymarked routes take
you on a circular navigation of
beech and conifers, scrub and old
oak woodland.

There is a longer, occasionally muddy route but the surface of the all-ability trail is superb. This offers good views and, half-way round, the wood opens out onto the edge of the hill from where you can enjoy vistas across Shrewsbury and the Welsh mountains beyond.

It's a wonderful place to enjoy being part of a vast landscape while sheltering from the elements.

The Ercall
Wellington

Take the Wellington turn off the A5/M54 and follow the signs to the Wrekin and Little Wenlock on B5061. Follow signs to Buckatree Hotel. Car park is on right in entrance to reserve.
(SJ640097), 53ha (131acres) SSSI
Shropshire Wildlife Trust & Borough of Telford & Wrekin

An atmospheric 'hanging wood' with evidence throughout of its ancient woodland origins.

Famed for its geological exposures, these are helpfully explained via a series of interpretive boards. The wood is interspersed with quarries, some of which are dangerous and therefore barred to the public.

Sandy soils here favour sessile oak with an understorey of heather, bilberry and mosses. Where the soils deepen, the oaks are replaced by hazel, ash and holly and, in the wet valley bottom, by alder.

In spring, the lower slopes are awash with bluebells, wood anemone, wood sorrel and yellow archangel, all ancient woodland indicators.

The bird population includes green woodpecker and sparrow hawks – smaller birds use the disused quarries for feeding and shelter in winter. Green and purple hairstreak butterflies can also be seen.

MAP 3

Severn Gorge & Coalbrookdale Woods
Ironbridge

From A4169 at Telford take B4373 to Ironbridge. These woods can be accessed from several points along the Ironbridge gorge.

(SJ694032), 270ha (667acres), SSSI

Severn Gorge Countryside Trust

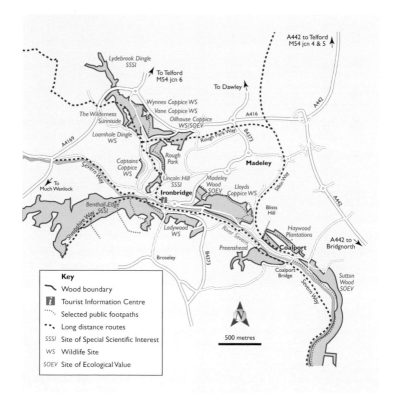

Severn Gorge

In order to do this justice, you would need to take a couple of days to explore the cocktail of woods and the rich industrial heritage of the area.

Many and varied, the woods that collectively make up the site belong to various owners and include Lydebrook Dingle, Vane Coppice, The Wilderness, Sunniside, Oilhouse Coppice, Lloyds Coppice, Madeley Wood, Captain's Coppice, Ladywood and Workhouse Coppice – see next entry.

Fortunately there is a wealth of information available including leaflets outlining some self-guided walks from the Severn Gorge Countryside Trust, but perhaps worth prioritising is Benthall Edge, a designated site of special scientific interest.

The area's natural assets – limestone, ironstone, sandstone, coal and clay – were harnessed by man and provided a huge boost for the area's industrial development.

All around as you wander through the woods, there is evidence of the impact man has had on the land and on the wood, with tall cooling-towers looming overhead, old lime kilns, clay workings, tramways and limestone quarries.

The climb through these hanging woods can be daunting, so sturdy boots are a must, and the rewards include some wonderful glimpses over to the other side of the gorge as you clamber up steep steps.

Benthall Wood itself divides into two distinct geological areas. The western part, mainly calcareous, supports species such as ash, yew, spindle as well as sycamore, hazel, oak and beech.

In contrast, the eastern side is acidic with underlying coal measures and oak growing in proliferation with birch, rowan and cherry. Benthall Edge is home to two of Britain's rarest native trees, the wild service and the large-leaved lime.

Workhouse Coppice
Ironbridge

From Ironbridge follow signs for B4373 crossing the Severn, then right into Ironbridge Road, left up the hill along Quarry Road and first right into Spout Lane. Main wood entrance 400 metres (0.25 mile) on right. Space for one or two vehicles on opposite side of road.
(SJ667029), 5ha (12acres)
Woodland Trust

Local residents and visitors alike make good use of the ancient woodland site of Workhouse Coppice, part of a larger wooded landscape overlooking the town of Ironbridge (see previous entry).

The site, which also overlooks the village of Broseley, is dominated by oaks dating back almost 100 years and a shrub layer of holly.

The site was historically used to help provide timber and charcoal during the early days of the Industrial Revolution and there are still signs of mine workings on the site, in the form of bell pits. Look, too, for an old sandstone quarry in the northeast corner of the wood.

A public footpath bisects the site and a number of smaller paths radiate from it, including one which links to Benthall Edge Woods.

Wenlock Edge
Much Wenlock

Runs for 30 km (18 miles) between Ironbridge and Craven Arms. From Much Wenlock take B4371 west. Wenlock Edge runs roughly parallel to this road, with several access points/car parks clearly signed.
(SO612997), 240ha (593acres), AONB, SSSI

The National Trust

A landscape feature teeming with lime-loving plants, mosses and liverworts, this ancient broadleaved site is a 'chocolate factory' for botanists.

Among the 'goodies' waiting to be savoured are dramatic views, rare flowers, fossils, limekilns and historic quarries – a real haven for wildlife.

Positioned on top of the limestone escarpment of Wenlock Edge, this is a site that's worth taking plenty of time to explore.

Ancient woodland survives on slopes too steep for agriculture. Today you will find bee orchid, herb Paris and spurge laurel amongst the glorious list of plant life.

The diverse habitats support buzzards, sparrow hawks and kestrels which breed along the scarp and in the summer, hobbies visit. Other woodland birds include woodcock and wood warbler. Ravens are regularly seen, as are marsh tits and great spotted woodpecker. 29 species of butterfly have been found here too.

Wenlock Edge

MAP 3

Helmeth Wood
Church Stretton

Take B4371 east of Church
Stretton towards Much Wenlock,
first left into Watling Street South
then right fork into Cwms
Lane. After 500 metres (0.25 mile),
there is a stile on right with public
footpath signs. Follow to top of
field and over stile into
wood. There is no parking available
on nearby lanes.
(SO469938), 24ha (59acres), AONB
Woodland Trust

An important landscape feature in
the heart of the Shropshire Hills
Area of Outstanding Natural
Beauty, Helmeth Wood adorns
Helmeth Hill, just half a mile east
of Church Stretton.

The underlying volcanic rocks
have evolved into a steep-sided
ridge with rocky outcrops, adding
interest to this ancient woodland.
Oak dominates the very steep
north and northeastern slopes.

Damp, acidic soils also sustain
birch, ash, and alder while, along
the base of the northern slopes the
rich ground cover is dominated by
bluebell and Yorkshire fog, a legacy
of heavy sheep-grazing in the past.

A public footpath leads into the
wood and through its southwest
section. Visitors can follow a
circular path, which gets quite
steep and wet in places, to explore
the wealth of ancient woodland
species from small-leaved lime and
toothwort to yellow archangel and
wood sorrel.

Helmeth Wood

Bury Ditches
Bishop's Castle

Located on a country lane between Clunton and Lydbury North, the woodland is signposted from the B4365 and B4385. (SO334839), 290ha (716acres), AONB

Forestry Commission

A commercial plantation set high up on a hill, this is a site with a wild, remote feel to it and panoramic views across great rolling landscapes. A visit here is an exhilarating experience.

Shafts of light create a wonderful scene with lots of verdant greens, yellows and reds. The surrounding hillsides are clothed in woodland and small farms nestle in the valley bottoms.

While planted conifers dominate, you can discover heather, bilberry, broom, hazel and rowan coppice, beech and oak.

It's just a short walk up the hillside to an Iron Age hill fort – still intact – where sheep graze and you can enjoy a 360 degree panorama across the hills of Wales and Shropshire.

Three well-signed routes aid access and the well-made forest track provides a cycle way right through the forest.

Hopton Wood
Craven Arms

Off B4385 near the village of Hopton Castle. From village follow minor road west until reaching forest on hill to left. Take small track left through farmland to car park. (SO355783), 338ha (828acres), AONB

Forestry Commission

Beautiful countryside with wide, open views of the South Shropshire hills and forest . . . this is the setting for Hopton Wood.

Mainly coniferous, the woodland sits on the side of a hill, towering over the village of Hopton Castle.

Norway spruce, Douglas fir and larch dominate with small areas of oak and beech, interspersed with 32km of forest roads and tracks. A clearly marked map helps guide you around.

This is a superb site for cyclists, with five colour-coded routes across varied terrain.

If you are looking to combine your visit with other sites, Bury Ditches and Clunton Coppice are both nearby.

Mortimer Forest

Mortimer Forest
Ludlow

Take the B4361 from Ludlow to Richard's Castle, cross the Ludford bridge and right into Wigmore Road following brown tourist sign. High Vinnalls is 4.5km (3 miles) on left.
Black Pool car park (off B4361 at Overton) (SO497717), High Vinnalls car park (SO474732), Whitcliffe car park (SO494742) 950ha (2348acres), SSSI
Forestry Commission

An ancient woodland site and former Saxon hunting forest, Mortimer is home to a unique breed of deer – long-coated descendants of fallow deer introduced by the Normans.

If possible, cycle through this huge forest – this allows time to climb to the summit and enjoy some fantastic views.

There are miles of well-maintained rides and three waymarked trails leading from the High Vinnalls car park: an all-ability trail, the three-mile Vinnalls Loop and the nine-mile Climbing Jack Trail.

The latter trail takes you through some of Britain's most beautiful countryside, across pastures, into the forest, with its feeling of isolation, the smell of countless conifers – and ventures high into the hills. The views here are spectacular with some wonderful vistas over verdant countryside to the Welsh hills.

There are also waymarked trails from both of the other car parks: Whitcliffe Loop Trail which takes you across the top of Mary Knoll Valley to look out over Ludford Park and Black Pool Loop Trail through historic Haye Park.

Croft Woodlands
Leominster

From Leominster take B4361 north towards Luston. 3km (2 miles) after Luston turn left on to B4362. Follow signs to Croft Castle. (SO452656), 52ha (129acre), SSSI

The National Trust

Anyone looking for a sanctuary from today's high-tech, high-speed world should visit this out of the way and incredibly peaceful wood.

Part of the 1,500 acre Croft Castle Estate – renowned for its Iron Age hill fort, fish pools and panoramic views across to Wales – it boasts some massive veteran trees and pollarded oaks both in the woods and within the parkland.

Once a deer park, the site is famed for its avenue of oak, lime and sweet chestnut – the latter of which is a sight to behold. Look for patterns in the twisted and gnarled bark – they are almost a work of art.

Managed as a productive, multi-purpose forest, the site is also well tended for conservation and recreation and has an extensive network of paths and tracks.

Croft Woodlands

MAP 3

Easters Wood
Leominster

From public car parking facilities in Leominster walk out of town on Bromyard road. After approx 400m (0.25 mile), at sharp right, follow public footpath down the side of public house car park, up steps over railway line, over footbridge, around field edge and under bypass. Wood entrance just after underpass.
(SO505589), 7ha (17acres)
Woodland Trust

Once arable and pasture land, Easters Wood is a new woodland which was planted in 1999 with native broadleaf trees.

Just five minutes' walk from the busy town centre of Leominster, the site is easily accessed via a public right of way which crosses both the River Lugg and the railway line.

Its boundary hedges are well stocked with mature broadleaves and the River Lugg site of special scientific interest marks its southern boundary.

Once inside, the developing woodland features an area next to the river planted with alder, ash, crack willow and black poplar.

Its eastern side is drier, containing ash, pedunculate oak, wild cherry and field maple. Wide, grassy ride edges are lined with shrubs including hazel, hawthorn, guelder rose and wayfaring tree. Elsewhere there are open glades, all of which can be explored via a network of permissive paths.

Brockhampton
Bromyard
Take A44 Bromyard to Worcester road. Follow brown tourist sign off
this road, a few miles to the east of Bromyard.
(SO687545), 176ha (435acres)
The National Trust

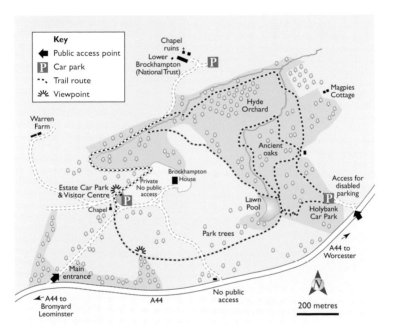

MAP 3

The magnificent, awe-inspiring woodland at Brockhampton is a feat, managing to look well cared for yet untouched by man at the same time.

Wonderful, majestic, hidden . . . the landscape unfolds gradually as you first descend the long drive to the hall and takes in some wonderful veteran trees standing proudly in the parkland.

The house is surrounded by orchards where members of the public can join in picking fruits during the season.

It's possible to walk for miles across grand landscapes or wander along tracks and well-signed, occasionally steep and muddy paths, staring in wonder amid the magnificent high forest and tall veteran oaks.

Families in particular enjoy the sculpture trail where you can look out for artworks hidden among the mixed deciduous and coniferous woodland.

In autumn the peace is interrupted with intermittent acorns falling to the ground or the occasional bird or mammal moving among shrubs and trees. Rotting trees are left where they stand or lie to provide sustenance for ferns and other epiphytes.

There is a shorter walk via the lawn pool, an area of open water which adds to the beauty of the site. Occasional benches are positioned thoughtfully, allowing regular stops to enjoy breathtaking, well-managed woodland.

Brockhampton

MAP 4

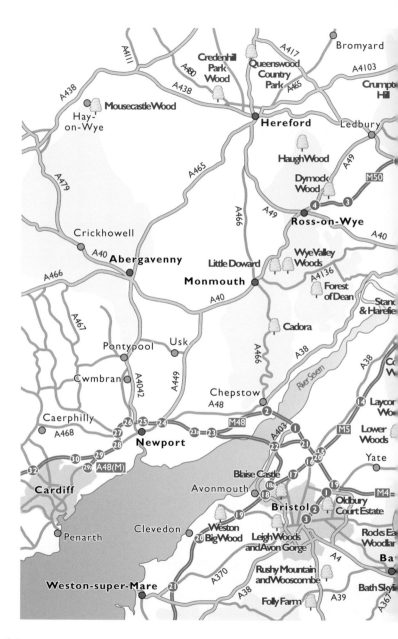

MAP 4

Tiddesley Wood
Pershore

From B4084 (formerly A44) just
north of Pershore take minor
road signposted to Besford and
Croome. Car park 800m (0.5 mile)
on left. (SO929462), 80ha (198acres)

Worcestershire Wildlife Trust

Tiddesley is a wonderful place for a
walk, whatever the season.

This ancient woodland site lies on
a small hill and as you explore, via a
network of gently undulating paths
and teasel-lined rides, the sound of
busy roads which surround the site
fade, giving way to birdsong and a
plethora of butterflies and insects.

Wooded since the last Ice Age, it
is thought, the site was used for
timber production in the past and
in the 1950s, part of the site
was replanted with conifers to
increase supplies.

Today it is managed for nature
conservation with a mixture of
oak, ash, hazel, birch, small-leaved
lime and shrubs including
blackthorn, guelder rose and
spindle. Wild service trees are also
found, along with wild pears, crab
apples and wild plums. In fact, the
original Pershore egg plum was
discovered in Tiddesley.

On a cautionary note, the
southwest corner of the wood is
used as a firing range.

Crumpton Hill
Great Malvern

Heading north towards Worcester
on A4103 turn right in Storridge
onto B4219. At first sharp bend
turn left down unsigned single
track lane. After 500m (0.25 mile)
look for footpath sign on right
between two houses into
orchard. Parking possible on verge
but take care not to block access
to drives. Walk down left side of
orchard to gated wood entrance.
(SO760488), 2ha (5acres),
AONB, SSSI

Woodland Trust

No fewer than 22 tree and shrub
species can be found packed into
this site of special scientific interest
in the heart of an Area of
Outstanding Natural Beauty.

This small ancient-woodland site
is one of a series dressing the
ridges of Wenlock limestone north
of the Malvern Hills.

The main woodland canopy is
high forest sessile oak but ash,

cherry and downy birch also grow here together with wild service tree, a feature of the site which is found in abundance. Some of the boundary trees are 200 years old.

The rich ground flora includes violet helleborine, herb Paris, dog's mercury and yellow archangel.

While the wood's north and western sections are generally driest, the southern end features several springs. An orchard has been planted on land to the south.

Queenswood Country Park
Hereford & Leominster

On the A49 between Hereford & Leominster, heading south, Queenswood is well signed on right. (SO506515), 68ha (168acres)

Herefordshire County Council

Packed with more than 450 varieties of trees from all over the world, the still-developing arboretum at Queenswood Country Park alone makes a visit worthwhile.

In spring be delighted by displays of flower-filled glades in the arboretum. You can let your imagination run wild, picturing what height the redwood grove might reach 1,000 years from now.

There is lots to discover in the park. The well-managed, and easy-to-access woodland – venue for an active events programme – supports a host of different bird species, including warblers and woodpeckers while insects, birds and amphibians live in seasonal ponds.

Another area worth exploring is South Woods, where oak grows alongside small-leaved lime and wild service trees and is home to a growing dormouse population. Make a beeline for the special viewpoint to enjoy panoramic views across the Malvern Hills and the Black Mountains.

Queenswood Country Park

MAP 4

Credenhill Park Wood
Credenhill

Leaving Hereford on A438 Brecon road, turn right immediately past entrance to Wyevale nursery onto A480, signed Credenhill. Straight over roundabout then second turning on right (heads almost back on itself) following brown tourist sign. Large car park 200m on left. (SO450445), 91ha (225acres)

Woodland Trust

A local landmark and historically important, Credenhill Park Wood is a large planted ancient-woodland site visible from Hereford, a few miles away.

Set in the central Hereford Hills, the site overlooks Credenhill itself and, because of its importance as ancient woodland, has been designated a special wildlife site.

Dominated by conifers, the wood includes 13 hectares of ancient semi-natural woodland including a small area of alder. Much of the ancient woodland flora still grows here, including early purple orchids, wild garlic and bluebells.

An integral – and significant – area of the wood is taken up by one of the largest hill forts in the Central Marches area – Credenhill Iron Age hill fort, thought to be one of England's 12 largest. Indeed, the site is thought to have been an Iron Age tribal capital.

Mousecastle Wood
Cusop/Hay on Wye

Follow B4348 east of Hay towards Bredwardine. After 800m (0.5 mile), at end of straight section, take unsigned turn on right at top of sweeping left-hand bend. Take next left, after 1.5km (1 mile), down unsigned single track lane. Follow to end where you'll find a gate into wood. Parking possible on verge but take care not to block access to any drives. (SO246424), 21ha (52acres)

Woodland Trust

A well-known feature of the local landscape, Mousecastle Wood clothes the steep east and south-facing slopes of an ancient scheduled monument.

The site includes areas of semi-natural ancient woodland, featuring mature oaks which lend the interior a dark and atmospheric look.

Elsewhere birch, ash, wych elm, sweet chestnut, sycamore, beech and wild service tree can be found. Hazel is widespread, offering a welcome nut harvest each autumn.

The site is well-served with permissive and public rights of way, providing walkers with a linear route through the wooded landscape.

Haugh Wood
Hereford

Haugh Wood is signed 1.5km (1 mile) from Midford village off the B4244, south-east of Hereford. (SO592365) 375ha (927acres)
Forestry Commission

Haugh Wood

This site ranks in the country's top ten habitats for invertebrates and is a wonderful place to see and learn about butterflies.

Situated on a hilltop, it features two wonderful butterfly trails laid out along forest rides. Interpretation boards explain about the butterflies visitors might spot.

The route takes you along well-made tracks that lead through conifer plantation, high oak forest and remnant hazel coppice.

A pleasant surprise awaits – a wildflower meadow, owned by Plantlife, can be seen at the northern edge of the wood.

Other areas have been opened up to create habitats for local butterfly species such as the pearl bordered fritillary, with the added benefit of providing extensive views of the surrounding countryside.

On the rides there is lots to look out for – including peacock and ringlet butterflies, buckthorn and hazel plus silver birch, oak, Scots pine, rose, willow and even small-leaved lime.

Dymock Wood

Dymock Wood
Kempley Village
From junction 3 of the M50 head
north on minor road to Kempley,
then turn south to Kempley
Green. Car park on left after
800m (0.5 mile).
(SO637285), 501ha (1238acres),
SSSI

Forestry Commission

Dymock Wood belies the Saxon
origins of its name – meaning dim
or dark oak wood – for it is
anything but dark. Rather the
reverse.

This diverse, well-managed site is
inviting and peaceful, despite the
fact that the M50 cuts through its
heart, and is well known for sheets
of wild daffodils each spring.

Much of the wood is managed
commercially – producing some
2,000 tons of timber per year –
while other sections, such as the
ancient semi-natural woods, Betty
Daws and Greenaways, are
managed for nature conservation.

Hay Wood and Shaw Common
are high forest grown from
coppice since 1840. They are also
the best areas to see the wild
daffodils in March

Variety extends across the nature
reserve which includes fen, marsh,
streams, ponds and heathland. The
end result is a beautiful – and
bountiful – landscape
complemented with orchards and
superb hedgerows.

While there are two waymarked
routes, a good sense of direction
would be an advantage.

Little Doward
Monmouth

North from Monmouth on A40 take exit at first bridge signed Ganarew, Crockers Ash and Doward. Follow road over bridge and A40 to Crockers Ash. Turn right for Biblins, following narrow road right turning onto Forestry Commission track, past Doward campsite to small car park 100m on right.
(SO548157), 82ha (203 acres), SSSI, AONB
Woodland Trust

Part of the nationally important Wye valley woods, Little Doward is a landmark with immense character, diverse species, great views and archaeological and geological interest.

Its varied geology and management have helped create a varied mix of habitats, some thought unique to the site. Little wonder it's very popular with locals.

A large part of the woodland is designated of special scientific interest and its historical links are impressive, as a large hill fort with Bronze Age barrows testifies.

The flanks of the hill are clothed in ancient woodland. Other sections mix conifers with non-native broadleaves, while limestone outcrops support notable flora and fauna species, including the nationally rare whitebeam tree. Greater and lesser horseshoe bats roost in its limestone caves.

To enter, take the path from the car park downhill to King Arthur's cave and follow the public pathway along the woodland boundary carrying straight on when the path turns sharp left for the river.

Little Doward

MAP 4

Forest of Dean
Coleford

Signposted off the B4226, west of the Speech House Hotel.
(SO615121), 11,000ha (27,227acres)

Forestry Commission

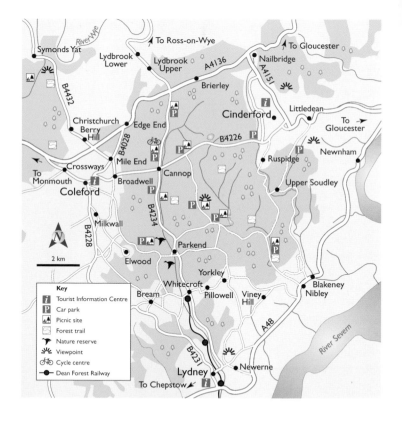

Near Parkend, Forest of Dean

If you ever yearn to lose yourself in nature make a beeline for this former royal hunting forest lying to the west of the River Severn. At 35 square miles, it's large enough to explore for weeks.

Its origins as a hunting ground date back to the Battle of Hastings and the death of King Harold, after which it was requisitioned by William the Conqueror. The oak woods on the western side of the forest derive from the grand oak first planted in the 11th century, though much of this timber was felled for ships during the rise of the Empire.

Its hunting days may be over but there is a huge list of other activities in this action-packed and dynamic environment.

From cycling and horseriding to birdwatching, running and orienteering, the forest is alive with opportunities. Add to this list caving, canoeing, climbing and even art appreciation – along a special sculpture trail – and entertainment.

Walking is well catered for with a series of waymarked routes ranging from short strolls to long-distance paths and all-ability trails. A good place to start exploring is Beechenhurst Lodge, which has a visitor information centre, café, shop, play area and picnic site – and lots of organised events.

Hugely popular with families, the forest has quite an enclosed feel to it. But this is a working forest with timber production at its heart and in its history.

Wye Valley Woods

Wye Valley Woods
Coleford

From A4136 Monmouth to
Gloucester road follow Symonds
Yat brown tourist signs from
junction with B4228 north of
Coleford. From A40 Monmouth to
Ross road, turn off at A4137
junction and follow brown signs.
(SO563160), 1234ha (3049acres)

Forestry Commission

Dramatic tree-clad cliffs and
majestic landscape views lie before
you on a visit to the Wye Valley
Gorge between Goodrich Castle
and Chepstow.

The extensive High Meadow
woods cover an area from
Symonds Yat Rock, down towards
Monmouth and across to the
villages of Christchurch and
Staunton. Tiddenham Chase sits in
the Wye Gorge off the B4228
between Coleford and Chepstow.

The woodland is well-signed and
well-served with pathways and
facilities. The sight of peregrines
soaring on the thermals below as
you watch from atop a 400ft cliff
proves a real draw.

This is the place to enjoy a
gentle stroll through the woodland
to the cliff top where an RSPB
watching area, on Forestry
Commission land, offers the
chance to enjoy the view of the
peregrines, as you look down onto
the meandering river and wonder
at the majesty of the landscape.

More woods to visit in the Wye
Valley appear in the Exploring
Woodland guide to Wales (due
Autumn 2006)

Cadora Woods
Monmouth

South from Monmouth on A466,
pass through village of Redbrook
and continue for approximately
5km (3 miles). Just before Bigsweir
Bridge take very sharp turning left
and follow minor road for 500m
(0.25 mile). Car park on left.
(SO545060), 112ha (277acres),
SSSI, AONB

Woodland Trust

Cadora Woods

The look, character and richness
of Cadora Woods, part of the
striking landscape of the lower
Wye valley, is in the process
of change.

   Among its most notable features
is a rich collection of old trees,
thought to derive from the
original natural woodland and
packed with archaeological
features.

   A section of the site – Bigsweir
Woods, is a site of special scientific
interest while Causeway Grove is
an ancient coppiced woodland
now mainly dominated by
sycamore. Look for trees with
multiple trunks rising from
their base – evidence of
former coppicing.

   Restoration of the site to its
former glory is already taking
place. This is important as it forms
a vital link with two other semi-
natural woodlands, increasing the
area's value as a vibrant and
dynamic wildlife habitat.

MAP 1

Lineover Wood

Lineover Wood
Dowdeswell

Two options. 1) just east of Charlton Kings off A40, look for large public house 'The Waterside' and wood entrance sign. Turn into gravelled track and follow to gated entrance to wood. Park on side of track, ensuring gate and other access points not blocked.
2) Heading east on A436,

Air Balloon to Andoversford road, wood and parking on left. If road side pull-in by locked gate is full continue east for 100m to large pull-in on left.
(SO987189), 50ha (124acres), SSSI, AONB
Woodland Trust

With a population that includes three deer species, foxes, badgers, and an abundance of ground flora and butterflies, Lineover is a wood of outstanding wildlife importance.

A network of interlinked but contrasting landscapes and habitats, including a meadow of species-rich limestone grassland, draws visitors throughout the year.

Small streams run through the woodland and underwater springs on the wood's mid-slopes help feed Dowdeswell reservoir.

The boundaries of the wood boast a number of features from bryophyte-supporting stone walls to wildlife-abundant hedgerows and wood banks.

The Cotswold Way national trail crosses the site, as do three other public rights of way.

Barber Wood

Barber Wood
Coberley

At Air Balloon public house roundabout follow A436 toward Cheltenham then first right down unsigned single-track lane. Take almost immediate right into single-track, rough surfaced lane with gated entrance to workshop (right) and gated field entrance to wood (left). Park either side of track in front of gates to wood. Ensure access to workshop drive is left clear.
(SO950158), 39ha (96acres), AONB
Woodland Trust

Lying 3 miles south of Cheltenham, Barber Wood straddles a large hill and forms an important part of the landscape in the Cotswolds Area of Outstanding Natural Beauty.

The woodland is a mixture of young mixed-broadleaf plantation and open limestone grassland with a rich and diverse population of species.

Sheep graze on the northernmost field while phased planting sees a young woodland developing at staggered ages.

Its prominent position affords Barber Wood a series of strong viewpoints – looking both out and in. The site also boasts a number of historic landscape features, including round clumps of mature parkland trees – roundels – and dry stone walls.

A number of majestic pollarded trees on the southern boundary date back more than 200 years.

MAP 4

Popes & Buckholt Woods
Stroud

Take lane off the A46 behind the Royal William public house, 3 km (2 miles) northeast of Painswick. (SO832086), 113ha (279acres), SSSI, AONB

National Trust & English Nature

This large site is part of the Cotswolds Commons and Beechwoods National Nature Reserve (NNR), where you will find some of England's best beech woods and limestone grasslands.

Buckholt NNR, by far the larger section, is steeped in history. During the 12th century it was used for hunting and was once owned by the monks of Gloucester.

Here, amid a mix of beech, oak, ash, holly, sycamore and hazel, buzzards soar above the trees, silver-washed fritillary butterflies feed on violets, and stinking hellebore grows on thin limestone soil, flowering in late winter.

Neighbouring Popes Wood is an ancient woodland. Set on a steep hillside, it's characterised by long, tall beech trees with ash and sycamore regeneration beneath and is being managed for both timber production and conservation.

Access is via a good network of stone bridleways and paths that can get muddy in places.

Standish Wood

Standish Wood & Haresfield Beacon
Stroud/Edge

From Stroud take A4173 to Edge.
Turn left just before Edge onto
minor road and continue until car
park on left is reached.
(SO819078), 152ha (376acres),
AONB, SSSI

The National Trust

You can choose between nature
and history when selecting a route
through this mixed beech site – a
great place to go for fresh air,
stunning views and a good,
long walk.

The woods themselves are very
popular but thanks to their sheer
size, have an open and uncrowded
feel to them.

A two-hour circular route
provides the chance to enjoy a
variety of species from beech,
honeysuckle, ivy, holly and ash to
conifers, hazel and hawthorn.

The woods, much of which were
cleared in the 1920s to make way
for beech, provide a spectacular
show of bluebells in the spring.

And what of history? Most
people flocking here head for the
Iron Age hill fort of Haresfield
Beacon, with its stunning view
over the edge of the Cotswold
escarpment and the Severn Vale and
Forest of Dean. There is also a
Neolithic chambered long barrow
in nearby Randwick Wood.

MAP 4

Frith Wood

Frith Wood
Stroud

Located 5km (3 miles) north of Stroud. Head north on B4070, going through Slad village until Frith Wood above on your left merges with the road, and you see Bulls Cross Common and crossroads. Immediately right is a layby. Cross over and walk back to the reserve gate entrance. (SO875085), 25ha (62acres), SSSI
Gloucestershire Wildlife Trust

A rather unkempt entrance belies the treats that await visitors who venture into the heart of this ancient woodland site.

Having survived wholesale clearance of woods in the late 20th century, this semi-natural beech wood has an abundance of species that confirm its age – including bluebell, sanicle, wood anemone, wild strawberry and wayfaring tree.

Choose from one of two routes to explore – the main bridleway is mainly level while the northern loop is quite steep. It's worth noting that both are muddy in parts.

One very interesting inhabitant to look out for en route is the rare woodland snail, Ena Montana, which has lived here since prehistoric times. It thrives among shade-loving plants such as white hellebore and common wintergreen which grow beneath the dense high forest canopy.

The name 'frith' gives a clue that by Saxon times, the wood was being used for charcoal-making, fence and firewood production.

Parish & Oldhills Wood
Stroud

Leave Stroud on A419 towards Cirencester. Leave Chalford up a steep hill, when road sweeps round to right turn left onto single track lane. Crossing canal bridge, turn right at T junction. 800m (0.5 mile) past playing field, at far end of wood, look out for double gated entrance and park alongside bollards.
(SO909030), 16ha (40acres), AONB
Woodland Trust

Well used every day by local residents of nearby Chalford and Frampton Mansell, this ancient semi-natural woodland is one element of a cocktail of habitats making up the local landscape.

The woods are dominated by beech high forest with a scattering of ash and oak and a rich tapestry of hazel, holly and yew beneath.

Oldhills Wood was felled shortly after World War Two while Parish Wood retains a high forest canopy of much older trees.

On the woodland floor you can find a rich floral population including species typical of the region's ancient woodland sites – amongst them ramsons, bluebell and spurge laurel.

The eastern edge adjoins Three Groves Wood, an ancient woodland site managed by Gloucestershire Wildlife Trust. Also adjoining is a privately owned and nationally recognised limestone grassland area with the delightful name of Strawberry Banks nature reserve.

MAP 4

Siccaridge Wood
Stroud

5km (3 miles) from Stroud on
A419 heading to Cirencester turn
left to Sapperton. Continue to
next crossroads and turn left. Go
past village & down hill. At bottom
park on left in small layby
(room for 3 cars).
(SO939034), 27ha (67acres), AONB
Bathurst Estate

Easy to navigate and great for a
pleasant walk, Siccaridge Wood sits
on the northern side of the
Sapperton valley.

The wood is an ancient semi-
natural woodland that sits on a
limestone spur between Holy
Brook and the River Frome.

Rich in life, the wood is a haven
for beetles, butterflies, moths,
spiders and snails and its large
anthills house up to 300,000 wood
ants. Adders are occasionally seen
bathing in the sunlight.

Ash, hazel, birch, beech, spindle,
hawthorn, wild service and small-
leaved limes abound. Sections of
ash were once felled to make way
for conifers but there are now
signs of healthy regeneration.
Wildflowers such as wood
anemone, bluebell, and lily of the
valley are all benefiting.

Occasionally steep, stony and
muddy paths and a deep drop
from the canal towpath make
careful supervision of dogs and
children essential.

Siccaridge Wood

Woodchester Park
Stroud/Nailsworth

On A419 southwest of Stroud take B4066 signed to Selsley and Uley. Follow brown tourist sign indicating car park on left of B4066. (SO827023), 204ha (504acres)

The National Trust

Hidden away from the rest of the world, this is a magical wooded valley, its tranquillity broken only by the sound of overhead gliders, buzzards and coots in the lakes.

It makes a large, sweeping and graceful descent into the valley leading to what looks like an archetypal haunted mansion. Unfinished, it nevertheless looks very imposing from the outside.

Venture past the house and a choice of three different routes take you either through the well-managed woodland or to a series of water features along the valley bottom.

Within the woodland, strong ash trees reach for the sky and you can stand back to admire some veteran beech. Making your descent through the valleys you look down onto these trees.

From dark coniferous forests you emerge to find yourself bathed in bright sunlight in a glade or meadow, surrounded by tall herbs.

Penn Wood & Stanley Wood
Stroud

Follow B4066 southeast out of Stroud toward Dursley. 300m after crossing Selsey Common turn right into large pull-in with double gated entrance. Either park in front of closed left-hand gate or enter woodland through open gate and park by bollards. Access both woods from here. Stanley Wood can also be accessed along B4066 a further 1.5km (1 mile) towards Dursley. Large lay-by on right opposite glider club entrance.

(SO821024), 68ha (168acres), AONB

Woodland Trust

Largely ancient, this substantial mixed woodland clings to the steep, north-facing slopes of the Cotswolds and, geologically speaking, is the best place in the county to view the scarp.

It sits within the Cotswold Area of Outstanding Natural Beauty and is believed to support a number of unusual plant,   ▸▸

113

MAP 4

bryophyte and invertebrate species along with bat roosts.

The woods are a mix of planted conifers, a pre-war larch plantation and high-forest beech but there is a rich mix of regenerated ground flora and understorey typical of the area.

The heart of the site is used as a scout camp and activity centre and a series of paths, including the Cotswold Way national trail, cross the woodland, ensuring good public access.

Neighbouring Stanley Wood continues the scarp woodland while, to the east, Selsey Common offers superb views over the Severn estuary.

Coaley Wood
Uley/Stroud
Follow B4066 north of Uley. After 800m (0.5 mile), pull into large layby on left. Gated entrance to wood at bottom end of lay-by, identified by Woodland Trust sign. (ST786998)
22ha (54acres), AONB, SSSI
Woodland Trust

The steep tree-covered slopes that dominate the skyline form a prominent, kilometre-long landmark on the edge of the scarp within the Cotswolds Area of Outstanding Natural Beauty.

Coaley Wood, part of a mosaic of semi-natural habitats, is an important haven for the rare greater horseshoe bat. This is just

Coaley Wood

one of a host of wildlife species including pearl-bordered fritillary butterflies, jackdaws, lizards, badgers and muntjac deer.

Close to the wood are three scheduled ancient monuments and a section famous for fossils.

The Cotswold Way national trail runs through the wood, which is criss-crossed by paths, bridleways and rights of way.

Areas of the site were felled in the 1950s and 60s to make way for a conifer-broadleaf mix, though few conifers remain and around half the woodland is covered with semi-mature high forest canopy. The rest has mature beech remnants and a dense understorey.

Laycombe Wood
Wootton-under-Edge

Leaving Wootton-under-Edge northeast on B4058, turn first left taking you sharply back on yourself into London Road (single track lane). Turn is not signed. On reaching farm buildings on left look for public right of way crossing road. Park on verge taking care to ensure no gates or drives are blocked. Follow path away from farm buildings between two tall hedges. After 50m path joins woodland edge from where you can turn left or right to enjoy Laycombe Wood.
(ST763954), 49ha (121acres), AONB
Woodland Trust

This long, thin strip of woodland sits on the steep, west-facing scarp slope of the Cotswolds.

An important landscape feature, the wood is a popular walking venue with locals, who visit daily.

From the top of the slope you can enjoy views across a number of landmarks including the Severn estuary, Tyndale monument and Waterly Bottom.

Inside, the site is made up of conifer plantation and beech high forest, the natural woodland cover. Conifers now account for about half the site and include blocks of Douglas fir, larch, Norway spruce and Scots pine.

Typically of beech-ash woodlands, the open ground and rides have developed a mix of herbs and flora indicating this as an ancient woodland site. Roe deer, grey squirrels and badgers animate the wood, with fine displays of common spotted orchids peppering the glade.

MAP 4

Westonbirt Arboretum

Westonbirt Arboretum
Tetbury

5km (3 miles) southwest of
Tetbury on A433 , Tetbury to Bath
road. 20 minutes northeast of
junction 18 of M4. Follow brown
tourist signs.
(ST854900), 240ha (593acres)
Forestry Commission

If anyone compiles a 'must see' list
of British woodlands, here's a site
that has to be on it. Full of awe
and excitement, Westonbirt is truly
a place for all seasons.

One half of the National
Arboreta ('other half' is Bedgebury
in Kent), the picturesque site was
created in 1892 by Robert
Holford and is managed today by
the Forestry Commission to
provide a relaxing day out among
some of the oldest, tallest and
rarest shrubs and trees in England.

There is a huge expanse of
woodland where you can wander
for miles along rides, drinking in
the sight of blankets of spring
bluebells, countless varieties of
trees with stunning spring and

autumn colours and participate in a choice of events.

In winter the woodland is dramatically floodlit. A host of innovative exhibitions and collections allow you to pore over 18,000 trees and shrubs from around the globe which have earned the site international acclaim.

In all there are 17 miles of pathways. These allow access to a host of landmarks such as Savill Glade, an area of former farmland where, in 1892, Robert Holford planted his very first tree.

Other key features include a 2,000-year-old lime coppice; Palmer Ride where you get a feel for the wildness of ancient woodland and Silk Wood with rare native wildflowers; or the Acer Glade – where you can admire the most famous maples in the country.

A trip to the café, forest shop and plant centre completes your visit to Westonbirt.

Midger Wood
Nailsworth

Take A46 south from Nailsworth for 11km (7 miles) turning right at Hillesdley sign. 700m (0.25 mile) down the hill, past grass field on right, park in small quarry on left. Walk down track on right and cross stream on footbridge. (ST794892), 9ha (22acres), SSSI

Gloucestershire Wildlife Trust

If you have a yearning to discover the magic of nature, don't miss Midger Nature Reserve.

This stunningly beautiful woodland, in a secluded valley seems almost beyond the reach of the modern world.

Even the risk of wet feet – access is across a stream – is worth it. Inside this ancient, semi-natural woodland twisted oaks, dripping with honeysuckle and ferns, mix with ash and field maple and an understorey of dogwood, wild privet and spindle.

In the flowering season enjoy the colours of early purple orchid, bluebell, herb Paris, wood anemone and green hellebore. In May, you might hear song thrush, blackcap, robin, blackbird and tree creeper to name but a few.

The moist atmosphere of the site provides a habitat for lots of fungi and the rare ancient-woodland snail Eva montana. At one end are flowers typical of limestone grassland – including rock rose, clustered bellflower and horseshoe vetch.

117

MAP 4

Lower Woods
Wickwar

From M4 exit 18 follow A46 north for 9.5km (6 miles). Turn left to Hawkesbury Upton, go through village and carry on to tall Somerset Monument. Fork left opposite on lane signed Wickwar, 5.5km (3.5 miles). Cross cattle grid, and across common to Lower Woods. Turn left opposite sign for Inglestone Farm, down track to Lodge.
(ST749885), 200ha (494 acres)
Gloucestershire Wildlife Trust & Avon Wildlife Trust

A vast site – at more than two miles long – and wooded since prehistoric times, Lower Woods is a giant gem with impressive links to the past.

This massive woodland, clearly seen from the Cotswold edge, is one of England's largest oak-ash woods but is actually made up of 23 distinct woods. Varied and fascinating, it has so much to explore, from grasslands, springs and geological exposures to the Little Avon river and a wealth of wildlife.

The woods are steeped in history – the Romans built a villa here where Saxons later settled – and boast, at 71, the highest number of ancient woodland indicators anywhere in the southwest.

Navigating such a large site is quite a challenge but there are three interconnecting waymarked routes ranging from one to two miles offering lots of chances to explore the wonderful array of trees including willow, alder, buckthorn and hazel.

Blaise Castle
Bristol

From A4 Portway, between Bristol and Avonmouth, turn right into Sylvan Road (A4162) to Sea Mills. Turn left at traffic lights into Shirehampton Road leading to B4057 Kings Weston Road. Car park is 1.5km (1 mile) on right.
(ST558788), 67ha (166 acres)
Bristol City Council

Every member of the family can find something to enjoy on a visit to the dramatic wooded parkland of Blaise Castle.

A registered historic park and garden with plenty to capture young imaginations, the estate was landscaped by Humphrey Repton. His talents can still be enjoyed

View to Goram's Chair, Blaise Castle

throughout the winding drives, footpaths, cottages and caves that enhance the natural beauty of a deep limestone gorge.

Explored via widespread paths, the estate boasts some spectacular views and lots of historical interest including Lover's Leap – a dramatic precipice – and an impressive rock formation called Goram's Chair.

This is a popular site, especially at weekends, when it's good to escape the crowds via the smaller footpaths that disappear into the woods – but don't forget your maps.

For an extended walk, nearby Kingsweston House boasts a mature woodland. Lime avenues line the old carriageway to the house which commands spectacular views from the edge of the ridge.

119

MAP 4

Oldbury Court Estate
Bristol

Take Junction 2 off M32 and follow signs to Fishponds. Just after passing church on left take left into Oldbury Court Road.
(ST635766), 29ha (72 acres)
Bristol City Council

If you are looking for a great day out for the family, head for Oldbury Court, an historic parkland with wonderful woodland that's perfect for children who like to explore.

The estate, like contrasting Blaise Castle on the western side of Bristol, was laid out by Humphrey Repton to maximise the stunning views across the River Frome gorge.

Its semi-natural woodland lines the deep-cut sandstone gorge to create a beautiful landscape with cliffs and outcrops clothed in mature trees and young, regenerating beech and ash.

A wide, level path echoing the route of the river is great for exploration but the steep climb makes this prohibitive for the less able. The more adventurous visitor can tackle the minor paths that clamber the steep sides of the gorge.

The woodland is made up of ash, beech, sycamore, oak, hazel, cherry and lime which help to support a variety of wildlife.

Rocks East Woodlands
Bath

From the north: M4 junction 18, take A46 south to A420. Turn left on A420 to Marshfield and then right into village and follow road towards Colerne for 5km (3 miles). Woods are on right. From Batheaston take Bannerdown Road towards Colerne. At Hunters Hall turn left onto Marshfield Road. Woods are 300m on left.
(ST775706), 40ha (99acres), AONB
A G Phillips OBE

What is believed to be Britain's tallest crab apple tree – at 62ft – is just one of a host of features to keep interest levels high in this woodland overlooking St Catherine's Valley in the Cotswolds Area of Outstanding Natural Beauty.

A unique management programme simultaneously encourages timber production, conservation, recreation opportunities and education.

This gets the most out of the mix of larch and spruce along with ash, beech, sycamore, oak, yew, field maple and giant redwood.

Several waymarked trails include a route down the valley to a restored woodland garden – passing by the giant crab apple –

and entering through the Valley of the Rocks.

The garden includes an ancient stone circle thought to be a sacred site and used today for blessings, handfastings etc. There is also a grotto, possibly dating back to Roman times, a pond and a cave.

Brown's Folly
Bath

From the A46 follow signs to Bathford. Past village of Bathford on minor road to Kingsdown, take steep right to Monkton Farleigh. Car park near brow of hill on Prospect Place.
(ST794660), 38ha (94 acres), SSSI
Avon Wildlife Trust

Hugging the hillside, high above the River Avon, Brown's Folly is home to rare plants and a nationally important bat roost.

Here you'll discover a rich mix of habitats with deciduous and coniferous woodland, rare limestone grassland and bat caves – and ample well-trodden paths to explore them.

Limestone was mined here from Roman times to the 20th century. Extensive remains of Bath-stone quarries provide a host of habitats

including Monkton Farleigh mine which has eight different species of bat including the greater horseshoe.

The area is also home to nationally rare plants – Bath asparagus and stinking hellebore, while wild thyme, harebell and nine species of orchid thrive on the grassland. The damp cliff-faces support a fascinating variety of ferns and fungi while pockets of ancient woodland on the lower slopes are home to woodpeckers.

Brown's Folly

MAP 4

Bath Skyline
Bath

There are various access points to the walk and limited parking (often with time restrictions) in some areas. Park and ride is available from the university on Saturdays. (ST777630)
227ha (561 acres)
The National Trust

Bath Skyline, a 500 acre site of meadows and woodland, offers spectacular views of Bath and the surrounding countryside.

The six mile walk, in which the woodland plays a small but key part, offers the chance to explore this landscape, its history and wildlife.

Two of the most significant woods are Bathampton and Bathwick. The former is on a sleep slope dominated with ash, hazel and yew, while ivy, moss and hart's tongue fern grow beneath the dense canopy.

Rocky outcrops at the top of the hill were once quarried and signs of the quarry tramline can still be seen, though most scars left by the industry have been covered by woodland regeneration.

Bathwick Woods, planted in World War Two for timber production, features ash, oak and sycamore with wild garlic blossoming in spring and a variety of fungi, including King Alfred's cake, worth an autumn visit.

Folly Farm
Bishop Sutton

From A37 Bristol to Wells road turn onto A368 at Chelwood roundabout heading west towards Bishop Sutton. Folly Farm is 3km (2 miles) on left just before village of Bishop Sutton. Note, sign not easily visible from this direction. (ST610603), 101ha (250 acres)
SSSI
Avon Wildlife Trust

A really welcoming wildlife-rich site with spectacular views and well-marked trails, Folly Farm combines two woods and a species-rich meadow, managed for conservation.

The site was once a medieval deer park and boasts several surviving veteran oaks.

Dowling's Wood, an ancient woodland site, has been managed for centuries as hazel coppice and continues to produce charcoal and firewood.

Folly Farm

Bluebells, primroses and early purple orchids add their colour. Tawny owls, nuthatch and greater spotted woodpeckers can all be found and buzzards are often seen circling over the hillside. Take care as the paths can be muddy, steep and slippery when wet.

Lighter and more open is Folly Wood with ash, oak and Scots pine above woodland grasses and sedges.

Linking Dowling's with the high forest of Folly Wood, the meadows sustain butterflies including the rare marsh fritillary while providing wonderful rural views.

MAP 4

Leigh Woods & Avon Gorge
Bristol

Follow Forest Enterprise sign off A369 Portishead to Bristol road. Further car park at Paradise Bottom off A369. Take turning to Leigh Court. A forest road leads off this to the right – the road to Leigh Court continues ahead – there is a small car parking area here which provides easier access to Paradise Bottom.

(ST553739), 186ha (460acres), SSSI

The National Trust & Forest Enterprise

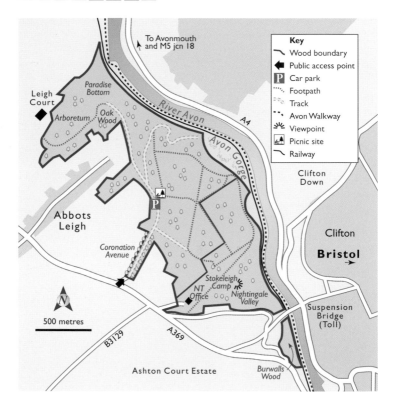

Leigh Woods is a wonderful blend of ancient woodland, 19th-century ornamental woods, remnants of wood pasture and 20th-century plantations. The site has evolved over centuries to create a landscape layered with history; a rich tapestry that is simply wonderful to explore.

Several waymarked trails offer good access of the woods, from a two-mile route along the edge of landscaped woodland through ancient woodland and recent plantations to a slightly shorter route leading to the edge of an Iron Age hill fort. There are longer tracks for cyclists which walkers can also explore.

Among the features of the ancient woodland are small-leaved lime and wild service trees and some species unique to the area including Bristol whitebeam, Bristol rock cress and Bristol onion.

One area of woodland, known as Paradise Bottom, was originally laid out as a woodland landscape garden in picturesque style, aimed at recreating wild and natural scenery. Over time this creation has been lost or damaged but restoration is now underway and it is possible to get a flavour of the original design masterminded by Humphrey Repton in the 19th century.

The woods are also renowned for their spectacular spring flower displays and have some lovely mature specimen trees, notably majestic evergreen Fulham oak and one of the first plantings of the Weymouth pine in this country, following its discovery in America. It all adds up to a delight for the whole family.

Avon Gorge

MAP 4

Rushy Mountain & Wooscombe Woods
Keynsham/Bristol

After leaving Whitchurch on the A37 going south take the first left signed Keynsham. After 1.5km (1 mile) fork right signed Woollard. After 800m (0.5 mile) fork left just before 'Publow' sign and then straight ahead at crossroads into Slate Lane. Car park 500m (0.25mile) on right.
(ST635653), 29ha (72 acres)
Brian Maggs

A young woodland, planted in 1994 in two neighbouring valleys, this site has already proved a big hit with local people.

Planted to form part of the Forest of Avon, the woods are easily explored via well-maintained paths and rides – and boast wonderful views across the surrounding countryside.

The trees include various broadleaves such as ash, oak, alder, birch, field maple, willow and poplar. There is a good variety of shrubs, too, with dogwood, spindle and wayfaring tree flanking paths and clearings.

The growth of the trees is uneven, reflecting the different ground conditions and microclimates in the two valleys. All adds to the interest and variety of a developing woodland.

While ladder stiles hamper access for less-able visitors, these may be removed in the future.

Weston Big Wood
Portishead

From B3124 Clevedon to
Portishead road turn into Valley
Road. Drive past civic amenity site
and park on roadside on left
opposite entrance to wood taking
care as this is a fast road.
(ST456750), 38ha (94 acres)
Avon Wildlife Trust

One of Avon's largest ancient
woodlands, Weston Big Wood
dates back to the Ice Age and
other historical remnants,
including medieval boundary
markers, can still be seen today.

The site is dominated by coppice
with oak, ash and hazel growing
along the top of the ridge while
small-leaved lime dominates the
slopes. Rare whitebeams and wild
service trees add interest.

Effective management of the site
has created rich and varied habitats
for a host of plants, insects and
birds – among them wood
anemones, violets and bluebells
which clothe the woodland floor
in spring.

Herb Paris, yellow archangel and
the rare purple gromwell can also
be found, and because the rides
are managed for butterflies there is
the chance to spot silver-washed
fritillary, holly blue and purple
hairstreak while woodland birds
include woodpeckers, nuthatches
and tawny owls.

A good network of sometimes
steep paths and rides weave their
way through dense coppice.

WOODLAND
TRUST

Trees and forests are crucial to life on our planet. They generate oxygen, play host to a spectacular variety of wildlife and provide us with raw materials and shelter. They offer us tranquillity, inspire us and refresh our souls.

Founded in 1972, the Woodland Trust is now the UK's leading woodland conservation charity. By acquiring sites and campaigning for woodland it aims to conserve, restore and re-establish native woodland to its former glory. The Trust now owns and cares for over 1,100 woods throughout the UK.

The Woodland Trust wants to see:
no further loss of ancient woodland
the variety of woodland wildlife restored and improved
an increase in new native woodland
an increase in people's understanding and enjoyment of woodland

The Woodland Trust has 150,000 members who share this vision. For every new member, the Trust can care for approximately half an acre of native woodland. For details of how to join the Woodland Trust please either ring FREEPHONE 0800 026 9650 or visit the website at www.woodland-trust.org.uk.

If you have enjoyed the woods in this book please consider leaving a legacy to the Woodland Trust. Legacies of all sizes play an invaluable role in helping the Trust to create new woodland and secure precious ancient woodland threatened by development and destruction. For further information please either call 01476 581129 or visit our dedicated website at www.legacies.org.uk

Autumn colour, Forest of Dean

Further Information

Public transport

Each entry gives a brief description of location, nearest town and grid reference. Traveline provides impartial journey planning information about all public transport services either by ringing 0870 608 2608 (calls charged at national rates) or visit www.traveline.org.uk. For information about the Sustrans National Cycle Network either ring 0117 929 0888 or visit www.sustrans.org.uk

Useful contacts

Forestry Commission, 0845 367 3787, www.forestry.gov.uk
National Trust, 0870 458 4000, www.nationaltrust.org.uk
Wildlife Trusts, 0870 036 7711, www.wildlifetrusts.org
RSPB, 01767 680551, www.rspb.org.uk
Royal Forestry Society, 01442 822028, www.rfs.org.uk
National Community Forest Partnership, 01684 311880, www.communityforest.org.uk
Tree Council, 020 7407 9992, www.treecouncil.org.uk
Woodland Trust, 01476 581111, www.woodland–trust.org.uk

Recommend a Wood

You can play a part in helping us complete this series. We are inviting readers to nominate a wood or woods they think should be included. We are interested in any woodland with public access in England, Scotland, Wales and Northern Ireland.

To recommend a wood please photocopy this page and provide as much of the following information as possible:

About the wood

Name of wood: _____

Nearest town: _____

Approximate size: _____ ha/acres

Owner/manager: _____

A few words on why you think it should be included:

_____

_____

About you

Your name: _____

Your postal address: _____

_____

_____ Post code: _____

If you are a member of the Woodland Trust please provide your membership number.

Please send to: Exploring Woodland Guides, The Woodland Trust, Autumn Park, Dysart Road, Grantham, Lincolnshire NG31 6LL, by fax on 01476 590808 or e-mail woodlandguides@woodland-trust.org.uk

Thank you for your help

Other Guides in the Series

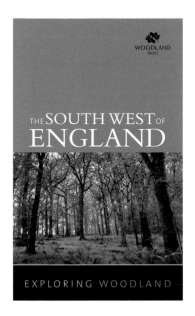

The South West of England
Published April 2006

Coming soon

The South East of England

The Peak District
and Central England

Wales

If you would like to be notified when certain titles are due for
publication please either write to Exploring Woodland Guides,
The Woodland Trust, Autumn Park, Dysart Road, Grantham,
Lincolnshire NG31 6LL or e-mail woodlandguides@woodland-
trust.org.uk

Index

Legal & General is delighted to support the Woodland Trust's conservation programme across the UK.

As a leading UK company, Legal & General recognises the importance of maintaining and improving our environment for future generations. We actively demonstrate our commitment through good management and support of environmental initiatives and organisations, such as the Woodland Trust.

Information on how Legal & General manages its impact on the environment can be found at www.legalandgeneralgroup.com/csr.